W9-CKU-567

The Hispanic Homograph

■ | ■ | ■

The
Hispanic Homograph

Gay Self-Representation
in Contemporary
Spanish Autobiography

Robert Richmond Ellis

University of Illinois Press
URBANA AND CHICAGO

Publication of this work was supported by the Program for Cultural
Cooperation between Spain's Ministry of Culture and Education
and United States' Universities

1 2 3 4 5 C P 5 4 3 2 1

This book is printed on acid-free paper.

Library of Congress Cataloging-in-Publication Data
Ellis, Robert Richmond.
The Hispanic homograph : gay self-representation in contemporary
Spanish autobiography / Robert Richmond Ellis.
p.   cm.
Includes bibliographical references and index.
ISBN 0-252-02311-0 (alk. paper). — ISBN 0-252-06611-1
(pbk. : alk. paper)
1. Spanish literature—20th century—History and criticism.   2. Gay
men in literature.   3. Autobiography.   4. Homosexuality and
literature—Spain.   5. Self in literature.   I. Title.
PQ6073.H65E55   1997
860.9'9206642'0904—dc20   96-35653
CIP

■

*"You guys are great in autobiographies,
but you really make me work hard."*
— Patty Diphusa

CONTENTS

Introduction

Gay Sexuality and Autobiography

Since the advent of multiculturalism in the 1980s, academic critics of literature have devoted increasing attention to issues of lesbian and gay sexuality. Just as anti-gay discrimination has come to be regarded as the unfinished business of the American civil rights movement, so the silencing of gay and lesbian sexuality in academic criticism and classroom curricula is being challenged as a final and necessary step in the reassessment and revision of the traditional canon of literature. For a number of professional readers, however, lesbian and gay sexuality remains at best a subject of secondary interest, obscuring what are deemed the more "universal" themes of literature. In parodying this attitude, Eve Kosofsky Sedgwick writes: "*Don't ask; You shouldn't know.* It didn't happen; it doesn't make any difference; it didn't mean anything; it doesn't have interpretive consequences" (53). Though such a position is clearly less prevalent in the academic world of the 1990s, discussions of lesbian and gay Hispanic and Latin American writing have been far from extensive, in spite of escalating enrollments in Latin American and Spanish literature courses and the proliferation of Latin American and Latino studies programs in American universities. Autobiography is particularly useful for gauging the ways in which modern sexuality can (and at times must) be represented and how sexual identity and sexual practice are defined, negotiated, and experienced in contemporary society. With this in mind, I have chosen to examine autobiographical texts of the following six Spanish writers: Antonio Roig, Juan Goytisolo, Jaime Gil de Biedma, Luis Antonio de Villena, Terenci Moix, and Pedro Almodóvar. In so doing I hope to shed further light on the theme of gay male sexuality in Spanish literature as well as to suggest possible avenues for future inquiry in the area of lesbian and gay Spanish-language writing in general.[1]

Theorizing Gay Sexuality

Since the coining of the term "homosexual" in the late nineteenth-century,[2] a debate has raged over the extent to which gay sexuality is an inherent essence or a fixed human nature and the degree to which it is socially and psychologically constructed. The so-called essentialist and constructionist positions were initially advanced by adherents of societal institutions and practices bent on containing or eradicating what was increasingly perceived to be a "homosexual problem": essentialism through the nineteenth-century medical establishment and constructionism within the framework of early psychoanalysis. The essentialist approach nonetheless came to dominate twentieth-century gay liberation movements and continues to be expressed by those activists (and scientists with a political agenda) who argue that lesbian and gay identity is not chosen, cannot be changed, and should hence be recognized as the foundation of a legitimate minority with the right to full participation in society and equal protection under the law. In contrast to essentialists, constructionists have directed their attention to the social conditions of lesbian and gay sexuality, distinguishing nuances of the largely reductionist claims of essentialism and relating the production of modern sexualities to the triumph of industrial capitalism. Both essentialism and constructionism have nevertheless tended in their own ways to universalize gay and lesbian identity, and whereas essentialism has led to an almost ethnic notion of gay sexuality (the "gay tribe"), constructionism, despite its historicization of the gay subject, has frequently relied for its data on a white, middle-class, male model.[3]

From the constructionist perspective, homosexual identity is a relatively recent phenomenon. Notwithstanding the ubiquitousness of homoerotic desire, premodern and early modern European societies did not equate sexual behavior with sexual identity. In sixteenth- and seventeenth-century Spain, as elsewhere throughout Christian Europe, sodomy was viewed as a freely chosen act of sin, rather than the consequence of a psychological or biological nature, and in his history of the persecution of sodomites under the Spanish Inquisition, Rafael Carrasco points out that according to the annals of the Valencia tribunals, inquisitors never once interrogated the accused about their sexual preferences or questioned if their sexual practices were exclusively homoerotic (134).[4] By the end of the nineteenth century, however, the theological conception of sodomy had been largely supplanted by biological and psychological discourses of deviance, and the apparatus was in place for a far more thorough policing of homoerotic activity. Barry D. Adam, along with a whole school of social constructionists, attributes this fundamental change to the economic exigencies of capitalism. He argues that heterosexual masculinity is the "embodiment" of the competitive egocentricity of the capitalist market system and that this system militates against homosexuality precisely because homoerotic bonding threatens the atomizing methods of domination (*The Survival of Domination* 56). Conversely, while capitalism rigorously enforces heterosexual masculinity among men, it makes possible the conditions for a lesbian and gay community: "In an entirely unexpected way, the lesbian and gay worlds developed with the rise of industrial capitalism, providing solutions on an individual, personal level to worker atomization" ("Structural Foundations of the Gay World" 664). This resulted primarily from the creation of new technology and the institution of waged labor, which freed men, and even more so women, from integrating themselves within traditional family structures.

Whereas constructionism examines the constructedness of gay and lesbian identities, poststructuralist theorization of gay sexuality, following in the wake of Derrida and Foucault, focuses on the interconnectedness of homosexuality and heterosexuality. Rather than discrete and self-sufficient identities, homosexuality and heterosexuality are conceived of, according to the Derridean model, as binary opposites, each inhering in the other as its logical contrary and subverting its ostensible autonomy. In the light of the Foucauldian genealogy of sexuality, this fundamental binarism becomes paradigmatic of the organization of power and knowledge within the capitalist state and more specifically the prototype of all modern sexual and social pairings. Although heterosexuality asserts itself as the dominant mode of sexuality under capitalism, it does so through the mediation of its homosexual contrary. Homosexuality in this sense is the sine qua non of heterosexuality. Repressive social, psychoanalytic, and pseudo-scientific practices might seek to eliminate homosexuality, but as Sedgwick suggests, they ultimately function to maintain and even foster it through the dynamics of the closet. The upshot is that identity politics, with its emphasis on lesbian and gay identity, is an equivocal enterprise, at least partially complicitous with the heterosexual hegemony[5] to the extent that it reinforces the indentitarian programs through which individuals are oppressed as lesbians and gay men. The poststructuralist critique of lesbian and gay sexuality hence abandons the external vantage point of both conventional pro-gay and anti-gay discourses and instead attempts to dislodge the inner logic whereby gay and straight identities are constituted in the first place.

As Steven Seidman notes, poststructuralism involves a shift "from the politics of personal identity to the politics of signification" (130). Its anti-identitarian impulse is the hallmark of a postmodernist worldview that has come to define itself as "queer." Traditional lesbian and gay male theory (whether essentialist or constructionist) presupposes a reification of desire that it takes as its object of inquiry. Queer theory, on the other hand, sets out to dereify desire, aligning itself with the oppositional sexuality that it elucidates while questioning its own role within the dominant sexual regime. It strives to recover neither a repressed psychic space (the latent homosexual) nor a mythical social sphere (the lost Lesbos or Sodom of a modern-day gay diaspora) and regards with skepticism any effort to "ground" sexual orientation, gender, or for that matter sex itself. Certain commentators inadvertently ossify the queer through the taxonomies of "queerness" or "queer identity," and as Michael Warner observes, "already people speak as though 'difference' were in itself a term of value. (It isn't)" (xix). From the perspective of the queer, difference is not even the exclusive heritage of those historically identified as different (i.e., lesbian or gay), and for this reason Alexander Doty rightly affirms a "straight queerness" (xviii) (although in so doing he too risks essentialism). Caroline Evans and Lorraine Gamman, bolstered by considerable feminist psychoanalytic theory, perhaps put it most aptly when they remarked that everyone is capable of his or her "queer moments" (6).

Nonetheless, if the queer, as Seidman suggests, is the by-product of a "poststructuralist critique of the logic of identity" that refuses "to name a subject" (132), what becomes of the concrete individuals who, *at least* at this moment in the history of capitalism, experience real oppression as lesbians and gay men? As Rosemary Hennessy clarifies, avant-garde queer theory, even when invoking a materialist discourse, erases labor from its social analysis (she speaks specifically of the post-Marxist Foucauldian approach of Judith Butler in *Bodies That Matter*). This erasure, she argues, results from the class position of academic practitioners of queer theory and leads to the assimilation of the queer critique within "hegemonic postmodern culture" (232). As Leo Bersani further contends, queer theory has simply failed to maintain its "gay specificity," which he distinguishes from "homo-sexual essence" (76). He points out that queer theorists have successfully ex-posed the disciplinary intent of identitarian discourses, but in so doing have lost sight of the gay and lesbian subject, leaving intact the heterosexist struc-tures they hoped to subvert: "We have erased ourselves in the process of de-naturalizing the epistemic and political regimes that have constructed us, [but] they don't need to be natural in order to rule; to demystify them doesn't render them inoperative" (4). Ironically, this de-gaying of gayness amounts to a "disappearing act" (5) and "accomplishes in its own way the principal aim of homophobia: the elimination of gays" (5). In response, Bersani advo-cates an examination of the "habit of desire" (6), which persists in spite of the deconstruction of identity. He conceives of homoerotic desire not as a lack that seeks fulfillment through the incorporation of difference (as occurs in "a psychology that grounds sociality in trauma and castration" [7]), but instead as a desire for a "seductive sameness" (150). This desire for sameness, or "homo-ness," is on the one hand "constitutive of community in that it tolerates psychological difference because of its very indifference to psycho-logical difference" (150). Yet on the other hand its "self-effacing" narcissism (150) is antirelational and anticommunitarian and hence for Bersani poten-tially more threatening to the given social order than the mere emptying of identity or the resignification of dominant configurations of gender and sexuality.

Bersani interrogates the poststructuralist axiom that sameness is of neces-sity internally mediated by otherness (as when Robert Young writes that it cannot even be thought except as differing from the different [88]). But is the expression of sameness, as he maintains, an antirelational and anticom-munitarian gesture? Or can it be a *joint* undertaking capable of deactivating, at least provisionally, the same/different, homo/hetero binaries? And is it possible to conceptualize sameness, not as a common, essential identity (the *idem*), but as a *practical position* of equality and action? With these questions in mind, I would like to attempt to shift somewhat the focus of debate from gay essence, or "homo-ness," to gay praxis, or what might be called the "homo-act."

In the homo/hetero binary, each term is mediated by its contrary, with the homo signaling the nonhetero and the hetero the nonhomo. In this scheme of "hetero-relationality" both the homo and the hetero are other-directed. Although an essentialist gay logic might endeavor to detach the homo from the binary in an effort to ground it in a hypostatized sameness, the homo remains "hetero-ized" through its internal contrary. Yet to the extent that the homo, as Bersani would have it, is "indifferent" to difference, the hetero can be bracketed. (Were the homo defined simply as "different from the different," then difference would perforce reappear in a pattern of infinite regress.) This indifference is not a passive structure of sameness but a homo-act that suspends difference and leads to a "homo-relationality." While in hetero-relationality the self and the other are rendered different through contrariety, in homo-relationality the self and the other, through their indifference to difference, tend toward similitude. Their homo-act, moreover, as the dynamic of homo-relationality, is ultimately not a desire of the masculine for the masculine or the feminine for the feminine, because masculinity and femininity, as master terms of hetero-relationality, are bound to each other as binary opposites. Instead, it is a desire for the unmediated self of the other, that is, of sameness for sameness, where sameness is understood as the homo-act itself. Homo-sex is precisely the concretization of the homo-act, and as such it can be viewed as the mutual (if fleeting) embodiment of sameness. In this sense homo-sex is neither narcissistic nor oppositional but reciprocal.[6]

Whereas hetero-relationality positions the self (either spatially, temporally, or logically) in opposition to the other (and in so doing delineates a "straight" line of demarcation), the homo-act "disorients" the self/other binary through its explicit indifference to difference. Its trajectory is "queer" in the etymological sense of "oblique," drawing sameness (forward and backward) through the self and the other. In contrast to hetero-relationality, which imposes an otherized sameness on the self and the other, the homo-act de-essentializes the self and the other by projecting sameness as a goal to be achieved. For this reason it constitutes what Ana María Alonso and María

Teresa Koreck, based on Donna Haraway's work, have called "affinity" (122) — that is, a movement toward a common end. The movement of the homo-act, though unidirectional, is polycentrist in origin, since it arises equally through two or through many homos. It is hence neither inherently oppositional nor inherently dyadic. In hetero-relationality, the self and the other are mired in an alienating essence, and their oppositions merely repeat and reaffirm the larger social antagonisms through which they occur. In homo-relationality, praxis is released from the atomized antagonisms of the self/other (where the slash separates while bringing the same to bear down on the other) and proliferates through the multiple and coextensive reciprocities of homo-homo-homo- (ad infinitum), which stand conjoined on equal and even footing. Given the overdeterminism of hetero-relationality as the dominant mode of sociality under capitalism, the homo-act is eventually reabsorbed in alterity, and sameness is made to recede on a horizon of selfhood. Yet the homo-act continuously reasserts a space wherein is possible not only the expression of homo-eroticism but also, significantly, the formation and mobilization of the homo-group.

The Practice of Autobiography

The construction of modern sexual identities and the institutionalization of autobiography as a dominant literary genre both take place within nineteenth-century bourgeois capitalism. Like early discourses of homosexuality, traditional autobiographical practice presupposes the existence of an autonomous self. It conceives of language, moreover, as an instrument of signification capable not simply of representing the self of the past but of recovering it and rendering the self of the present ontologically whole. Traditional autobiography thus aims to repair an egological dislocation wrought through the passage of time, and in this sense can be seen to function as an act of retotalization, at once synchronic and diachronic, of the multiple intentionalities of an individual consciousness. Rather than a simulacrum of life, it establishes itself as a site wherein a "life" is produced and historicized.

Autobiographical theorization, which dates from the pioneering work of Georg Misch, has historically regarded autobiography as a uniquely Western phenomenon, attributable according to Georges Gusdorf to a Western penchant for individualism (29), and has largely ignored the autobiographical practices of non-Western cultures. Although Misch sought the origin of modern autobiography in classical Greek and Latin writers, scholars of historical criticism usually identify the medieval Christian confessional as the prototype of the genre. Most histories of autobiography begin with the *Confessions* of Saint Augustine, whom William C. Spengemann maintains "set the problem for all subsequent autobiography: How can the self know itself?" (32). For Augustine, the instrument of self-knowledge is language. Augustine used language as an epistemic tool, but its consequences in the religious context of the *Confessions* are profoundly ontological. As Spengemann observes, Augustinian language is "the means by which grace is realized, instantaneously, in the present moment" (32). This attempt to achieve an ideal self through the medium of language is precisely what makes the *Confessions* paradigmatic of much subsequent autobiographical writing.

Needless to say, however, medieval confessionalists and autobiographers under bourgeois capitalism hold markedly differing conceptions of the nature of the self and its relation to the world. Confession is an explicitly relational enterprise. Confessionalists articulate their lives in reference to their confessors (in the case of Santa Teresa the mandated other of autobiographical intentionality) and ultimately God, through whom they derive not only their moral justification but also their very being within the created order. What is more, they recognize that their lives are internally mediated by a discourse, be it the dogma of the church or the divine Word itself. Bourgeois autobiographers, on the other hand, see themselves as the makers and proprietors of their lives and the uncontested arbiters of a personal truth for which they alone are responsible. Their writing thus both requires and reiterates the ideology of capitalism through its affirmation that an individual "life" is not merely possible but ultimately is a dimension of private property and at times even a source of capital itself.

It is a commonplace of autobiographical criticism that Spaniards and Latin Americans have historically produced fewer autobiographies than other Western Europeans and North Americans. Although the grounds for such a claim might be sought in the economic conditions of pretwentieth-century Spain and Latin America, critics have speculated on such diverse factors as racial temperament (the 1953 editors of *Revista de Literatura* in "Las zonas desérticas de nuestra literatura" 261); national psychology (Ortega y Gasset 156–57); a Catholic conception of life (Juan Carlos Ghiano, in Prieto 17–18n12); and a desire to shield the family from close public scrutiny (Woods xiv, xxii).[7] Despite the rigorous separation of the public and private spheres in traditional Hispanic society, Spanish and Latin American autobiography is in fact more thoroughly developed than previously maintained. Sylvia Molloy dismisses the assertion that "Hispanic writers, for elusive 'national' characteristics, are not prone to record their lives on paper" (2) and argues that the apparent dearth of autobiographies in Spanish America is the result of reader blindness: "The perceived scarcity of life stories written in the first person is less a matter of quantity than a matter of attitude: autobiography is as much a way of reading as it is a way of writing" (2).[8]

The French critic Philippe Lejeune was one of the first to address the agency of the reader of the autobiographical text, and in his authoritative, yet now highly contested treatise *On Autobiography* [*Le pacte autobiographique*], he elucidates the fundamental assumptions of traditional autobiography and establishes the conceptual framework that subsequent poststructuralist theorists have challenged. It is his contention that autobiography is founded on a claim not of historical exactitude but of sincerity that leads to a tacit agreement between reader and writer that he describes as an "autobiographical pact." Through the autobiographical pact the reader accepts as "true" both the supposed facts of the narrative and the autobiographical conflation of the writing subject and the subject of the written text. In this way the autobiographical pact reaffirms the referentiality of autobiographical discourse and the ontological integrity of the self.

The so-called truth claim, intended to distinguish autobiography (along with traditional historical discourse) from such "fictional" genres as the novel, becomes a major point of controversy in poststructuralist critiques of life writing. In his essay "Autobiography as De-Facement," Paul de Man applies Derridean deconstruction to the autobiographical genre, and in so doing denies the referentiality of the autobiographical text and the fixedness of its subject. From this deconstructive perspective, the subject of autobiography is never fully present insofar as its meaning is continually slipping from one signifier to another without ever anchoring itself in a final signification. This is the case not only with the written subject but with the writing subject as well since it too is constructed through language and is hence a fiction. Within Hispanic autobiographical criticism, Patrick Dust examines the

Vida of Santa Teresa in an effort to move beyond the traditional autobiographer's "naïve equation of aesthetic illusion with reality" (83) and the deconstructionist tenet that "all representation is misrepresentation" (85). He proposes that autobiography is *"both* half-full *and* half-empty" (91), thereby attempting to mediate what he sees as the deconstructionist draining of the self from autobiography and the traditionalist certitude of Barrett J. Mandel that autobiography is "full of life now." His analysis is similar to that of Paul John Eakin, for whom the autobiographical enterprise recapitulates "the fundamental rhythms of identity formation" (9). Eakin rejects the "either/ or proposition" of the self as a "transcendental category preceding language in the order of being, or else a construct of language brought into being by it" (8) and instead chooses "to conceptualize the relation between the self and language as a mutually constituting interdependency" (8) that is sometimes formally articulated through the autobiographical act. The middle path of Dust and Eakin is particularly useful in approaching lesbian and gay life writers, who often use autobiography as a primary means of identity formation, while revealing a keen awareness of how their lives have been overdetermined within a hetero-relational (and heterosexist) discourse.

According to Lejeune, the first gay autobiographies were composed in France during the latter half of the nineteenth century when the medical establishment, at the behest of legal authorities, sought the case histories of gay men to determine whether their actions were criminal or pathological.[9] The "delinquent/patient" agreed to recount his story, at times to attain a reprieve or a cure and at times in the hope of altering prevailing views and ameliorating the condition of gays in society. Lejeune cites one who writes:

J'écrirai, tant bien que mal, l'histoire de mes souffrances; je ne suis guidé que par le désir de pouvoir contribuer par cette autobiographie à renseigner quelque peu sur les malentendus et les erreurs cruelles qui règnent encore dans toutes les sphères contre l'inversion sexuelle. ("Autobiographie" 83)

[I will write, somehow or other, the story of my sufferings; I am guided only by the desire to be able to contribute through this autobiography to informing somewhat about the misunderstandings and cruel errors that still prevail everywhere against sexual inversion. (trans. mine)]

Lejeune proceeds to demonstrate that these autobiographies, as case studies, involved collaboration and compromise on the parts of both the gay writer and those in the legal and medical institutions. On the one hand the writer was obliged to enunciate his voice through a discourse that defined him a priori as socially, psychologically, and biologically deviant (if not simply nonexistent), while on the other hand those in the establishment risked allowing a testimony that might undermine the very ideology they endeavored to preserve. What is more striking is that gay life writing, like religious confession, evinces from the outset an intuition that the self exists only in and through language. It is for this reason, rather than on account of a facile equation of homosexuality with sin, that the narration of the gay life is frequently thought of as a confession. As Georges Hérelle, an openly gay writer and critical observer of nineteenth-century French medical practice, was perhaps the first to declare: "Nous avons tous une envie folle de nous confesser, de crier notre amour" (qtd. in Lejeune, "Autobiographie" 90) [We all have a mad desire to confess, to shout our love (trans. mine)].

The discursive tension of these early gay autobiographies is, according to the deconstructive analysis of Lee Edelman, the hallmark of gay inscription, or "homographesis." Homographesis, he theorizes, is a dual operation. Its first phase, which corresponds historically to the construction of homosexual identity within nineteenth-century medical and legal discourses, is regulatory in that it attempts to reduce difference to the determinate difference of the same. Its second phase, in contrast, is resistant to the extent that it exposes the difference internal to the same. The "inscription" of the homo is thus for Edelman a concomitant "de-scription" of identity. In keeping with the Derridean conception of writing, Edelman maintains that homographesis undoes identity precisely to the degree that identity can be articulated solely in relation to signs that are themselves structured by their own non-self-identity through an "inevitable exchange of meanings in the prefixes 'homo' and 'hetero'" (14). The initial objective of homographesis is to essentialize identity, but the "homograph" (for Edelman both a body and a written text, and as I will henceforth argue, what might be divided into gay autobiography, queer autobiography, and homobiography), confounds the distinction between difference and sameness. The upshot is that while heterosexuality strives to reify homosexual difference, homosexuality interjects difference within the same/different binary, thereby representing the difference *from* binary difference. Homosexuality in this way functions as neither the same nor as the different but as a "fissure" within the representation of sexual identity and the signifier of the impossibility of any identity that claims presence to itself.

Following the deconstructive argument of Edelman, it might be said that all autobiographies function as homographs. The writing (graph) of the self (autos), like the writing of the same (homo), is, according to Derrida, a "homonym" (8). Yet since sameness is forever dispersing into heterogeneity, autobiography might likewise be called a "heterograph," even though conventional generic studies limit the term "heterobiography" to those texts in which the writing subject differs explicitly from the subject of the written text (Winslow 30). As either hetero or homo, the autos is internally mediated by contrariety, and in this sense autobiography as a genre can be read as the formal articulation of hetero-relationality. It affirms a self (traditionally bourgeois, white, straight, and male) in opposition to the other, and while the narrative of its egological struggle tends to end in personal triumph, it typically leaves intact the antagonistic structures that formed the condition of its original conflict. This antagonism often remains present even in lesbian and gay life writing, although as revealed in several of the Hispanic texts of this study, the dynamics of homographesis significantly challenge the rhetorical structures of hetero-relationality within which it operates. What is more, these homographs make clear how the workings of gay sexuality must be taken into account in the formulation of any general theory of modern autobiographical practice.

Traditional autobiographers frequently highlight a crucial episode of the past through which they attempt to essentialize the heterogenous and disparate moments of their entire lives. In religious confessionalists this might be the experience of conversion: when Augustine hears an angelic voice bidding him to open and read from the book of the Apostle; in modern, secular autobiographies the *prise de conscience* takes a variety of forms: when Gibbon descends the Capitoline Hill, Rousseau ponders the value of scientific progress, or Yevtushenko observes the passage of Stalin's coffin (Shapiro 438–39; Weintraub 824). Lesbian and gay autobiographers are wont to describe the process of coming out as the decisive event of their lives and make it the primary focus of their autobiographies. Not only is coming out the master narrative of much lesbian and gay life writing, but the autobiographical text itself can function as the ultimate act of coming out inasmuch as publication brings the private lesbian or gay life into an unlimited public sphere. Coming-out narrators, like traditional autobiographers, look to their pasts, but there is a tendency on their part to reject their former lives as false and to turn within to what they perceive to be an unrealized self that exists solely in potential. As Diana Fuss remarks: "In both gay and lesbian literature, a familiar tension emerges between a view of identity as that which is always there (but has been buried under layers of cultural repression) and that which has never been socially permitted (but remains to be formed, created, or achieved)" (*Essentially Speaking* 100). Lesbian and gay autobiography might hence be viewed as constructionist to the extent that it seeks to produce a gay identity. But its underlying thrust is essentialist, since identity is not created but is instead realized through the actualization of a potential essence.

In fact the coming-out narrative, as an instance of homographesis, both resists and colludes with the heterosexual hegemony to the degree that the affirmation of gay and lesbian identity involves an implicit affirmation of its heterosexual contrary. Moreover, it does not destroy the closet but instead manifests its dual sidedness, and whether one is inside or out, the structures of hetero-relationality continually reassert themselves. Yet as Fuss maintains: "That hierarchical oppositions always *tend toward* reestablishing themselves does not mean that they can never be invaded, interfered with, and critically impaired" ("Inside/Out" 6). Queer writing works precisely in this way, and rather than effect a coming out, it strives to subvert dominant configurations of sexuality. Such writing, according to Julia Watson and Biddy Martin, represents lesbian and gay sexuality "as a transgressive desire and a provocation to heretofore unspeakable connections and affiliations," and in so doing frees lesbian and gay life writing from its own "generic orthodoxy, in the 'law' of the coming-out story" (Watson 144).[10]

Lesbian/gay and queer autobiography each delineate the two directions of homographesis, but with differing emphases. Gay/lesbian autobiography seeks to inscribe gay and lesbian identities, though its ostensible goal is not to regulate but to liberate the lesbian and gay male subjects. Its specific aims are the recovery and realization of a repressed and potential self. As revealed in gay male Spanish texts, however, it fails to the extent that its essentialism binds it to a hetero-relational structure through which it is inherently and incessantly hetero-ized. In contrast to lesbian/gay autobiography, queer autobiography makes explicit the second phase of homographesis through its stress on the "difference from difference." It neither affirms nor denies gay and lesbian identities but endeavors to destabilize all sexual and gender identities by allowing them to free-float across the hetero/homo and masculine/ feminine binary divides. Within the Spanish context, its modus operandi is camp. While gay/lesbian autobiography attempts to invert the hetero/ homo binary (a move that embeds it ever more deeply in hetero-relationality), queer autobiography works within the hetero/homo and masculine/feminine binaries, repudiating the ontologizing drive of lesbian/ gay autobiography as complicitous with the oppression of gays and lesbians and choosing to refigure the epistemic structures of gender and sexuality. But as the queer fiction of Pedro Almodóvar demonstrates, it too tends, as does queer theory itself, to erase gay and lesbian specificity. As Bersani writes with regard to homographesis, in queer autobiography "the value of 'acts of gay self-nomination' is thus exactly equivalent to their negativizing, self-destructing potential" (69).

Homobiography, as a third direction in lesbian and gay life writing, projects sameness rather than difference. Whereas queer autobiography interjects difference within the same/different binary, thereby reducing its subject to the negative sign of "the different from the different," the subject of the homobiographical text is "indifferent to difference." Homobiography is hence the formal expression of the homo-act. It neither "inscribes" nor "de-scribes" gay/straight identity but instead essays a provisional "description" of hetero-relationality and "inscription" of homo-relationality. In the process it retrieves the affirmative impetus of traditional lesbian/gay autobiography while simultaneously generating, in the wake of queer deconstructions, a politically efficacious homo-praxis. Furthermore, the homobiographical text affinitizes both the written self and its various others as well as the writing self and the reader. Homo-reading in fact gives rise to a "homobiographical pact," resulting neither from the presumed "authenticity" or "historical exactitude" of the homobiographer, nor even less so from an ontological subsumption of the writing and written selves, but from the degree to which homo-readers are able to dislodge hetero-relationality. Homobiography nonetheless avoids the "enchantment" of what Edelman calls the "phantom of a political engagement outside and above an engagement with issues of rhetoric, figuration, and fantasy" (21), and rather than ignore "the historical conceptualization of homosexuality in a distinctive relation to language" (21), it works within the "fissure" that Edelman equates with gay sexuality, rhetorically sighting (and siting) the space of a common homo-praxis.

Like queer autobiography, homobiography rejects the essentialism of gay/lesbian life writing. Yet its subject is conjoined with the other — not in a relationship of contrariety, nor through an ontological or epistemic bond, but through praxis. This praxis differs from the ludic performativity of queer autobiography in that it contextualizes itself in terms of concrete historical, social, and political tensions. At the present moment AIDS is the overdetermining condition of the homo-act and of all homos, both sero-positive and sero-negative, precisely because the positive/negative binary has itself been collapsed through a social discourse that conflates the gay male and AIDS bodies in an effort to reconfigure the traditional homograph, and through a process of "diseasing," literally to "ease away" the homo, albeit with devastating consequences. For this reason homobiography explicitly asserts the "bios" within the homograph. Although critics such as Domna C. Stanton have found it necessary to excise the "bios," with its facile and patriarchal assumptions of referentiality, in the hope of creating a more generous and dynamic living space for women (vii–viii), the "bios" of homobiography is not reducible to gender, nor to the "life" or "organism" that for Foucault is the construct and object of modern regimes of power. As Helen M. Buss suggests, it is also a "way" or a "course" (117–18), and in homobiography the "common way" of the homo-act. In "making their way," homobiographers plot the "bios," not only through an "inscription/de-scription" of AIDS as the sign of death (the "thanatos" being the ultimate "truth" of the hetero-ized homo), but also through the projection of an affinity, as Donna Haraway puts it, "related not by blood but by choice" (72). In doing so, they activate what Sartre has called a "fused group," that is, an unstructured collective of discrete praxes in which each is the concrete embodiment of the praxis of the whole (See Sartre, *Critique* 345–404). As the homobiographical text of Goytisolo discloses, one of the surprising effects of AIDS is the transformation of homosexuality from the ossified essence of atomized individuals into the dynamic of practical (and

...dical political) action. What is more, it envisions an affinity transcending the boundaries of gender and sexuality, as well as those of ethnicity and social class.

In the Spanish Context

Gay Spanish politics, and much of contemporary gay Spanish culture, reveals an anti-essentialist thrust similar to that of recent sexual and literary theorization. Whereas the Stonewall riots of 1969 (a concrete act of gay resistance to police oppression) mark the beginning of the gay liberation movement in the United States (though its actual origins precede this watershed year by several decades), gay liberation in Spain came to fruition in the liberal climate of the late 1970s and early 1980s as a consequence of the dissolution of the Franco regime. In contrast to its North American counterpart, Spanish gay liberation was initially perceived as part of a broad national movement of democratization, and from the outset proponents established solidarity with various constituencies, including heterosexual women, workers, and, in Catalonia and the Basque Country, regional political and cultural organizations. As Canadian Tim McCaskell comments: "The men who make up the vast majority of EHGAM [Euskal Herriko Gay Askapen Mugimendua/The Basque Gay Liberation Front] find their personal and political lives far more intertwined with lesbians and with straight people of both sexes than gay men are apt to in North America" (223).

The origins of Spanish gay liberation can be traced to the early 1970s when Catalán activists sought the repeal of the laws criminalizing gay and lesbian sexuality. In 1970 the government proposed replacing the 1933 Ley de Vagos (law of vagrants), which penalized certain sexual acts, with the more repressive Ley de Peligrosidad y Rehabilitación Social (law of social dangerousness and rehabilitation), according to which conduct even suggestive of a "homosexual nature" was deemed legally suspect. A 1971 amendment to this law called for the removal of gays to a rehabilitation center, a provision harking back to a 1954 statute that mandated their internment in labor camps. Through the pressure of activists, this legislation was modified, and more significant, the apparatus was set in motion for achieving the eventual depenalization of lesbian and gay sexuality, which occurred in 1978. A driving force was the Front d'Alliberament Gai de Catalunya (FAGC) (Catalán gay liberation front), which articulated much of the Spanish gay agenda during the period of transition from dictatorship to democracy.

The *Manifiesto* of FAGC, promulgated in 1977, stands as a foundational document in which its authors express their comprehensive agenda of gay liberation and delineate the scope of gay Spanish politics in the years prior to the onslaught of AIDS. As a post-Marxist liberationist tract, it was written to integrate the project of gay liberation within the larger ideological framework of class struggle. In so doing the authors dissociate themselves from the ethnic paradigms of gay sexuality advanced by the Anglo-American gay liberation movement of the immediate post-Stonewall period. The *Manifiesto* is noteworthy because the designation "gay"[11] is defined in it not as a positive rescription of the negatively constituted essence of homosexuality but as a move away from the essentialist categories homosexual/heterosexual, masculine/feminine, and even male/female. The *Manifiesto* can therefore be seen to anticipate the postmodern conception "queer." Its writers reject homosexual identity (which they implicitly distinguish from homoerotic desire) as an instrument intended to repress homoeroticism, "puesto que el mantenimiento de la «homosexualidad» como categoría separada va indefectiblemente unido a su represión" (*Manifiesto* 34; qtd. in Mirabet i Mullol 335) [since the maintenance of "homosexuality" as a separate category is indefectably united with its repression (trans. mine)]. Despite their anti-identitarian politics, however, members of FAGC predicated the *Manifiesto* on an overarching narrative of resistance and a millenarian vision that will be realized not within but beyond prevailing binary gender arrangements, through "una amplia lucha ideológica que tiene que ser asumida por la clase obrera a través de sus organizaciones de masas" (*Manifiesto* 34; qtd. in Mirabet i Mullol 335) [a broad ideological struggle that must be assumed by the working class through its mass organizations (trans. mine)].[12]

The first extensive Spanish treatise on gay male sexuality (intended as a defense rather than a denunciation of homoeroticism) is *Heraclés: Sobre una manera de ser* [Heracles: About a way of being], written by the poet Juan Gil-Albert in 1955 and published in 1975. As the title suggests, Gil-Albert adopts an essentialist stance insofar as he defines gay sexuality as a mode of being. He posits that the gay male is inherently masculine and that any expression of femininity on his part is the result of a misguided imitation of heterosexual norms. Although Gil-Albert would make masculinity an avatar of sameness among gay men, masculinity arises, whether homosexually or heterosexually, through its feminine contrary. He thus declares: "El amor sexual entre hombres no tiene nada que ver con la mujer y responde, precisamente, al deseo, bien manifiesto, de prescindir de ella" (86) [Sexual love between men has nothing to do with woman and responds, precisely, to the manifest desire to dispense with her (trans. mine)]. To say the least, this is an indirect apology of gay male love. For Gil-Albert, sex between men is first and foremost not an affirmation of masculine sameness but a denial of the feminine, and concomitantly of woman as the incarnation of the feminine. As such, it is intrinsically coiled, despite Gil-Albert's ostensible intentions, within hetero-relationality. As Jonathan Mayhew points out, Gil-Albert aims to legitimize gay male sexuality, but he ends by reinforcing a bias that privileges masculine bonding (or what Sedgwick calls "homosociality"[13]) and silences feminine affectivity and sexuality (132). Gil-Albert claims to detect in male homoeroticism an act of rebellion — "una rebeldía . . . contra la naturaleza, pero que levanta su grito inmemorial desde el trasfondo de la naturaleza misma" (190) [a rebellion . . . against nature, but that raises its immemorial cry from the background of nature itself (trans. mine)]. But this rebellion, regardless of its initial opposition to nature, is reabsorbed within the natural hegemony. As Edelman remarks of homographesis, it is hence a rebellion that "conserves what it contests" (14).[14]

Homoeroticism is present in much of the poetry of the Spanish Generation of 1927 with which Gil-Albert is loosely associated.[15] The most renowned of the period, Federico García Lorca and Luis Cernuda, represent gay sexuality in their writings,[16] but of the two only Cernuda identifies himself openly as a gay man. As Gil de Biedma notes, Lorca is the first in Spanish literary history to make the gay male the explicit subject of a published text (in such pieces as "Canción del mariquita" [Song of the fairy]), but he nonetheless distances himself from his gay personae (in Swansey and Enríquez 202–3). While this is not the case in the posthumously published *El público* [*The Public*] and the "Sonetos del amor oscuro" [Sonnets of dark love], Lorca is consistently uneasy in the face of what he perceives as a feminine homosexuality, and in the most celebrated of his gay-themed poems, "Oda a

Walt Whitman" [Ode to Walt Whitman], he rejects as promiscuous a certain effeminate gay male behavior. In so doing he implicitly affirms the same model of masculinity advanced by Gil-Albert and the deep-rooted homosociality, or what Gil de Biedma calls "homosentimentality" (with "homo" meaning masculine), of traditional Spanish culture (in Swansey and Enríquez 205). This is perhaps most apparent in certain poems of the *Romancero gitano* [Gypsy ballads] and "Llanto por Ignacio Sánchez Mejías" [Lament for Ignacio Sánchez Mejías].[17]

The writings of Lorca and Cernuda reveal the two phases of homographesis (crystallized in the Gil-Albertian articulation of rebellion) in that they both disrupt dominant patterns of sexual representation while simultaneously supporting an essentialism that ultimately functions to counter its emancipatory project. In the writings of Lorca, and in particular in *El público* (without doubt his most complex and suggestive gay-themed work), there is a decided emphasis on performativity, with its shifting sexual and gender roles. Yet the preeminent Lorquian image of the mask, like that of the closet itself, presupposes an inner/outer and, by extension, homo/hetero binary opposition. This binary, borne out not only on the thematic level of the play but also through the generic intersection within the Lorquian oeuvre of the theatrical and the poetic, reaches a critical moment in *El público* when the character of the Director declares:

> ¡Hay que destruir el teatro o vivir en el teatro! . . . Por eso yo me atreví a realizar un dificilísimo juego poético en espera de que el amor rompiera con ímpetu y diera nueva forma a los trajes. (155–57)

> [One's got to destroy the theater or live in the theater! . . . For that reason I dared to perform an extremely difficult poetic trick in hopes that love would impetuously rip the costumes to shreds and then give them a new form. (45)]

In this statement, the Director expresses a desire first to demolish the mechanism of his oppression and subsequently to refabricate it in a way that might reflect his inner, gay self. This self, however, exists solely in opposition to its heterosexual contrary, and the more he struggles to affirm the homoerotic "theater beneath the sand," the more the "open-air theater" of hetero-relationality exerts its power and reinforces the mask of alterity. He thus pronounces: "No hay más que máscara" (105) ["There's nothing but masks" (26)]. What is significant is that these masks are donned not in a ludic (and, given the numerous role switches, draglike) gesture that might loosen their grip, but rather in a deadly serious game in which the performer is increasingly alienated from an impossible authenticity, both through the heteroizing gaze of the public as well as from the antagonisms of gender and sexuality that overdetermine his own interpersonal relationships in the "theater beneath the sand." Though the Director concludes that nothing, save the desire for authenticity and death itself, lies hidden behind the mask, the mask remains, concealing an empty closet in which the gay male is finally silenced.

El público is weighted by what Sartre, in contradistinction to the "gay science" of Nietzsche, has called the "spirit of seriousness" (see Sartre, *Being and Nothingness* 796–97). This is the opposite of camp, which aims to lighten the burden of identity. Throughout *El público* the discourse of hetero-relationality retains its original power to oppress. This discourse, Lorca intimates, is forced on (and within) the gay male through an irreversible act of violence: "Yo vi una vez a un hombre devorado por la máscara. Los jóvenes más fuertes de la ciudad, con picas ensangrentadas, le hundían por el trasero grandes bolas de periódicos abandonados" (43) ["I once saw a man devoured by the mask. The strongest youths of the city rammed large balls of thrown-away newspapers up his rear with bloodied pickaxes" (5–6)]. The consequence of this rape, at once physical and discursive, is not fecundity but sterility.[18] In fact the gay male figures of *El público* can generate no reading but the official one ("la letra era más fuerte que ellos" [139]) ["the words were stronger than they were" (39)], and although they rebel, their rebellion (like that of their "in-drag" counterparts in the rural tragedies) is an "unproductive" gesture, short-circuiting and leading in the end to their own undoing.

The poetry and poetic prose of Cernuda is less queer than the poetry and theater of Lorca in that it lacks the sexual and gender reversals of such plays as *El público*. It is also more explicitly autobiographical.[19] Like Lorca, Cernuda attempts through a poetic act to articulate an unfettered, homoerotic desire, envisioning what might be called a gay utopia. As Gerardo Velázquez Cueto indicates in his analysis of the collection *Un río, un amor* [A river, a love], this gay utopia is first conceived of as a site of difference, where difference might ultimately lead to the realization of a mutual sameness (3). In the poem "Todo esto por amor" [All this for love], Cernuda speaks of a space

> Donde estrellas
> Sus labios dan a otras estrellas.
> Donde mis ojos, estos ojos,
> Se despiertan en otros.
>
> (*Poesía* 104)

> [Where stars
> their lips to other stars give.
> Where my eyes, these eyes,
> Are awakened in others.
>
> (trans. mine)]

In Cernuda, nevertheless, the self generated through the sameness of the other remains sterile, and as in Lorca is reabsorbed within hetero-relationality. As Velázquez Cueto observes, this results according to Cernuda not simply from the external determinism of a heterosexist society but through an incapacity and cowardice that gay men have historically internalized (3). Sameness in Cernuda therefore remains mediated by the difference through which it is initially posited, and as in Lorca the gay male is caught in a permanent dialectic of contraries. The poem "Dejadme solo" [Leave me alone], hence closes with the verses

> La verdad, la mentira,
> Como labios azules,
> Una dice, otra dice;
> Pero nunca pronuncian verdades o mentiras su secreto torcido;
> Verdades o mentiras
> Son pájaros que emigran cuando los ojos mueren.
>
> (*Poesía* 108)

> [The truth, the lie,
> Like blue lips,
> The one speaks, the other speaks;

> But truths and lies never pronounce their twisted secret;
> Truths or lies
> Are birds than migrate when the eyes die.
>
> (trans. mine)]

The "twisted secret" to which Cernuda alludes would be his authentic gay self. It is "twisted" precisely through hetero-relationality, and more specifically through language. As Velázquez Cueto explains, language for Cernuda is a mask. Like Lorca, however, the more Cernuda tries to dissociate himself from his masks, rather than ironize them from within, the more he conjures forth their power to alienate. He too calls for a rebellion: "Alzate y vé" (rise up and see), all the while aware that in his case rebellion leads nowhere: "aunque aquí nada esperes" ("Noche del hombre y su demonio" [Night of man and his demon], *Poesía* 334) (even though here you expect nothing; trans. mine).

While the writings of Lorca and Cernuda have been seen to contain autobiographical elements, they are actually more similar to autobiographical fiction than conventional autobiography per se. Openly gay autobiographies were not published in Spain until the latter quarter of the twentieth century,[20] and even then they were written largely by writers who came to maturity during or after the fifties, including Jaime Gil de Biedma (1929–90), Juan Goytisolo (1931–), Antonio Roig (1939–), Terenci Moix (1942–), Luis Antonio de Villena (1951–), and Pedro Almodóvar (1951–). These life writers engage in a wide range of autobiographical practices that encompass autobiographies, diaries, and memoirs as well as autobiographical fiction. To one degree or another, their conceptions of sexuality have been forged through and against the patriarchal and heterosexist assumptions of Francoism. Moreover, their social and cultural backgrounds as Spanish males vary considerably. The family depicted by Villena is aristocratic; those of Gil de Biedma, Goytisolo, and Moix are bourgeois (upper, middle, and lower, respectively); those of Almodóvar and Roig are working class. Whereas all write in Castilian, only Villena (Madrid) and Almodóvar (La Mancha) are Castilian by birth. Gil de Biedma, Goytisolo, and Moix were born in Barcelona, and Roig in Ibiza. In the latter three, sexual awareness as gay men was coupled with a growing awareness of cultural and linguistic difference within the dominant Castilian framework. Together, then, their texts not

only reflect regional and social diversity but also make explicit the interconnectedness of sexual identity and practice and language, culture, and class.

I have chosen to present these writers according to what I perceive to be
an increasingly anti-essentialist and ludic aesthetic and have grouped them
under the tentative rubrics of "gay autobiography" (Roig, Goytisolo, and
Gil de Biedma), "queer autobiography" (Villena, Moix, and Almodóvar),
and "homobiography" (Goytisolo). Rather than rigid generic categories
delimiting and containing autobiographical intentionality, I see "gay,"
"queer," and "homo" as conceptual tools useful for charting directions
within autobiographical discourses. Goytisolo, Gil de Biedma, Villena, and
Moix all oscillate between essentialist and anti-essentialist poles. Roig, in
contrast, insists on the fixedness of gay identity while Almodóvar dispenses
with gay identity altogether. Of the six, only Goytisolo produces what I envision as homobiography, not in his formal autobiographies but in a fictional (and like much of his fictional production), quasi-autobiographical
text published immediately following his autobiographical volumes. This
text is significant, for it both reconceptualizes the essentialist identity of gay
autobiography and resituates the ludic performativity of queer autobiography. In so doing it reaffirms the efficacy of gay male writing in a historical
and political moment of extreme crisis.

PART ONE

Gay Autobiography

CHAPTER ONE

Antonio Roig

In the Confessional Mode

I begin with the autobiography of Antonio Roig, not because it is exemplary of Spanish gay life writing but because it can be read as a kind of cautionary tale of the hazards encountered by the ostensibly well-intentioned gay or lesbian writer. Though Roig sets as his goal the affirmation of a positive gay identity, he ultimately reiterates the most heterosexist stereotypes of gay male sexuality. His inscription of gay identity not only "de-scribes" itself homographically but also is reabsorbed within a crushing hetero-relational discourse over which he has no control and within which he is able to exercise only the most minimal discursive maneuvers. This results primarily from the confessional mode that he unwittingly adopts. From his position as a Carmelite priest, Roig vociferously attacks the anti-gay bias of the Catholic church, seeking in Christianity and the Carmelite heritage of San Juan de la Cruz a tradition of tolerance through which gay-identified men and women might find inclusion. Yet the prevailing dogma of the church continues to haunt him, even after he is defrocked and expelled from monastic life. The authentic voice he seeks to utter is in fact no more than an echo of his "inquisitors," and its articulation, as Bersani so aptly writes of confession, is but a form of ventriloquism (12). Numerous gay life writers, from the North American Paul Monette to Goytisolo himself, see themselves at some moment in their lives as ventriloquists, but whereas Goytisolo manages to turn his voice into a medium of homo-reciprocity, Roig becomes the agent of his own isolation and eventual silencing as a gay man.

Identifying a Genre

The autobiographical texts of Roig, like those of many gay life writers, resist classification according to conventional taxonomies of autobiographical discourse. The title of his third autobiographical volume, *Vidente en rebeldía: Un proceso en la Iglesia* [Seer in rebellion: A trial in the church], contains no explicit reference to genre. The titles of his initial two volumes are followed by parenthetical subtitles indicative of a specific autobiographical subgenre: *Todos los parques no son un paraíso (memorias de un sacerdote)* [All parks are not a paradise (memoirs of a priest)] and *Variaciones sobre un tema de Orestes (diario, 1975–1977)* [Variations on a theme of Orestes (diary, 1975–1977)]. Strictly speaking, however, neither is *Parques* a memoir nor is *Variaciones* a diary. This is because each forms part of a larger autobiographical enterprise that, unlike the memoir, emphasizes a particular life over its social context, and in contrast to the diary, regards this life in its totality.

Whereas traditional autobiographers focus primarily on their individual lives, memoirists tend to view their lives as a means of revealing a larger social or historical milieu. By positioning themselves vis-à-vis their lives and their societies, they thus stand doubly removed from the day-to-day reflections of diarists. Diaries differ from autobiographies and memoirs insofar as their object is a single day rather than an entire life. Even if an autobiography is a mere compilation of diurnal occurrences, the perspective of the autobiographer is distanced from the past by a greater passage of time and is consequently more all-encompassing than that of the diarist. According to the generic paradigms of Georges May, the autobiographer performs an act of "rediscovery" (167), while the diarist actually attempts to discover the self. This might account for the tendency, indicated by Béatrice Didier, of many alienated women and gay men of the nineteenth century to practice the *journal intime* rather than autobiography proper.[1] It might also explain why Roig adopts a diary style in his moments of greatest self-doubt and anguish.

Both *Parques* and *Vidente* can be considered memoirs to the extent that Roig highlights the social context of his life as a gay man through lengthy meditations on the secular world of London and the religious world of the Spanish cloister. They were conceived of, however, not as commentaries on the status of gay sexuality in European society during the 1970s but as articulations, through the recollection of the most significant moments in a particular life, of a voice that is at once distinctly individual and inherently gay. *Variaciones,* nonetheless, is the most explicitly autobiographical piece insofar as it describes, through the medium of the daily experiences recounted, Roig's childhood and formative years. Although *Parques* and *Vidente* contain references to earlier episodes in his life, they concentrate primarily on time frames that are limited in duration and relatively close to authorial time. Specifically, in *Parques* Roig narrates the period 1972–75, when he lived excloistered in London. As with Goytisolo, this self-imposed exile is the condition of an un-closeting, not only of a repressed sexuality but of a voice heretofore silenced through a multifaceted (Castilian, Catholic, fascist, and masculinist) hetero-relational discourse.[2] The pivotal event indicated in the title occurs when Roig is entrapped and arrested during a sexual encounter in London's Hyde Park. In this moment his sexuality is seen and interpreted within the framework of hetero-normativity. What is significant is that Roig is "outed" in a public (and foreign) space precisely because he has no space of his own wherein to express his sexuality. Indeed, he is always on someone else's textual ground. Yet rather than devise a strategy for reworking this space and articulating a common ground of reciprocity with other gay men and women, he attempts to transcend it, though ultimately to no avail.

Roig is actually expelled from the Carmelite order and priesthood not on account of the Hyde Park incident, which inter-European police agencies bring to the attention of his superiors in Spain, but for publishing *Parques* without seeking the prior approval of ecclesiastical censors. The events surrounding his expulsion form the subject of *Vidente,* which covers the years 1977–78, after he reassumed his vocation and religious life. *Vidente* is thus the counterpoint to and conclusion of the *Parques* narrative.

In Search of a Voice

In *Variaciones,* which forms a hiatus between the completion and publication of *Parques,* Roig reflects on the epistemological and ontological structures of life writing. On one level he takes the existential position that life has no apparent a priori meaning and that as a writer he is simply "un testigo más de lo absurdo de la existencia" (*Variaciones* 31) [one more witness of the absurdity of existence].[3] In this context his task is not to reveal but to endow his life with meaning—"situar razones detrás de mi vida" (*Variaciones* 47) [situate meanings behind my life]. Despite its meaninglessness and degradation through meanings imposed by others, life for Roig is inherently valuable. He in fact sees in his autobiographical enterprise moral and even religious dimensions that he characterizes in terms of the mystical theology of San Juan de la Cruz. Writing, he declares, is a kind of dark night and an effort to unveil a light within the soul. Nonetheless, it is not a solitary spiritual act but a "compromiso vital" (*Variaciones* 31) [vital commitment] and a "servicio a la verdad y a los derechos de ciertas personas" (*Variaciones* 32) [service to the truth and to the rights of certain persons]. For Roig the inner light or truth is human freedom, an essence transcending the seeming absurdity of the human condition, and the "rights of certain persons" are those of gay men and lesbians.

Roig maintains that the development of his voice was thwarted in childhood and adolescence through the dominant language. Born and raised in Ibiza, his native tongue was not Castilian but Ibicenco. At the age of twelve he was sent to a seminary on the mainland and forced to use only Castilian.[4] Through the pro-Castilian dictates of the church and Francoist state, he was thus denied immediate access to his regional culture. Eventually, he lost his fluency in Ibicenco and was obliged to communicate with his family members in a language that was not their own. The loss of Ibicenco, however, was minor in comparison with the damage caused by the absence of literature in the seminary. There, the only books available to the young reader were the laws of the order and the Bible, both in Latin, and the writings of San Juan de la Cruz and Santa Teresa, though these, Roig contends, were presented in a manner that distorted and deformed their original meaning. The texts he read were largely part of a legalistic prohibition—an instrument of oppression that ultimately functioned to silence him. As a consequence, he actually lost the ability to write:

> En mi noviciado, sin hipérbole, me olvidé de manejar la pluma. . . . Las páginas que conservo del tiempo de mi filosofía muestran hasta qué punto me había atrofiado. La caligrafía es mala. Los rasgos, en vez de descubrir señales de personalidad, me delatan infantil y torpe. Mi imaginación estaba sometida por el miedo. Quería ser fiel a la maraña de leyes y normas y quedaba anulado. (*Variaciones* 134)

[During my novitiate, without exaggeration, I forgot how to use a pen. . . . The pages that I have kept from the time of my philosophy studies show the degree to which I had become atrophied. The handwriting is bad. The strokes, instead of revealing the traces of personality, betray my immaturity and awkwardness. My imagination was subdued by fear. I wanted to be faithful to a tangle of laws and norms and I ended up annulled.]

Only much later in youth did Roig discover writers in whom he thought he recognized his own stifled voice. It was then that he decided that he had been living his life against the grain and that in order to achieve authenticity he would have to turn back and disentangle his voice from those that had been thrust upon him:

Había errado el camino al seguir unas orientaciones que nunca había asimilado. Tenía que desandar lo andado y regresar a las raíces de mi persona. Desvelar mi propia voz y tener el valor de oírla: doliente, fresca y original. (*Variaciones* 135)

[I had taken the wrong path by following certain orientations that I had never assimilated. I had to go back to square one and to the roots of my self. To reveal my own voice and to have the courage to hear it: aching, fresh, and original.]

According to this passage, Roig conceives of his life as an exile, for which he himself is at least partly responsible, from an original and essential gay wholeness. Through his autobiography he will attempt an egological return, purging the alien voice of heterosexuality and releasing his repressed homosexual voice. This is clearly the aim of gay and lesbian life writing as traditionally practiced. Yet Roig's formulation of the gay autobiographical enterprise is unusual in that he foresees adopting a passive stance with regard to his gay voice. In the moment of truth he will listen rather than speak. Hetero-relationality will therefore not be deactivated but maintained through a self/other dichotomy lodged at the heart of unity. This in fact is the contradiction inherent in any project of "roots" or "origins."

In *Variaciones* Roig identifies his authentic voice with that of the classical hero, Orestes. Just as the latter murdered his mother so as to avenge the death of his father, Roig believes that he must suppress the voice of the maternal figure as he has internalized it and allow the paternal voice within him to speak. As an adult he views the voice of his mother as one of radical negation — she never wanted him to be born and she never loved him as a child: "¡Cuánto odio y aniquilamiento no soporté en su mirada! Había sido vomitado a un mundo hostil. . . . Soy el que no tenía derecho a ser" (*Variaciones* 245) [How much hatred and annihilation did I not endure in her look! I had been vomited into a hostile world. . . . I am he who has no right to be]. Although the voice of his father was presumably one of potential affirmation, it was silenced by his mother. The linguistic silencing experienced in the seminary was thus a secondary structure of a more profound ontological silencing originating in the primordial interiorization of maternal denial. Through a kind of Oedipal reversal, Roig strives to overcome this self-denial. In so doing, however, he mythologizes his father.[5] To a certain degree this accounts for his search for a paternal figure in his male lovers. It also reveals a narrow assessment of the role of women in Spanish family life. Rather than interpret the negativity of his mother in its larger social dimension, he chooses to regard her as wantonly cruel. He hence fails to realize the common structures of her alienation as a woman and his as a gay man in a hetero/sexist society. Moreover, despite the apparent suffocation of his voice, he is capable of writing, while she for all intents and purposes remains irremediably silent.

Like Gil-Albert, Roig elucidates a masculinist version of homosexuality. Specifically, he grounds gay male sexuality in a fundamental bond between the son and the father that is interrupted through the failed maternity of the mother. This reading of his childhood prevents him from clearing the egological slate, since it maintains intact the hetero-relational structures of gender. The voice of the mother might be stilled, but the voice of heterosexual masculinity, which constituted the condition of her negation in the first place, continues to reverberate within him and to obstruct his effort to achieve a pristine state of homo-origin. Through the guise of a latter-day Orestes, Roig actually reexerts the power of the heterosexual masculine other, and as a consequence his attack against the mother figure ultimately backfires on himself.

After the period of secularization in London, Roig returned to conventual life in Spain, believing that the moment had arrived for change within the nation and especially within the church. But as the incidents related in

Vidente reveal, the church was not prepared to realize the kind of changes that Roig had in mind. In *Vidente* his struggle to express an authentic gay voice is pitted directly against the dogmatic discourse of the church. Upon hearing at Mass a recitation of the Pauline text, "¡No os engañéis! Ni los afeminados, ni los homosexuales heredarán el Reino de Dios" (*Vidente* 23) [Be not deceived! Neither the effeminate nor the homosexuals will inherit the Kingdom of God],[6] he exclaims:

> Oh, Dios, defiende mi causa contra quienes escribieron los textos de Génesis y Levítico, de Romanos, Corintios y Timoteo; o de quienes al interpretar tales textos aplastaron mis esperanzas y me condenaron a ser extranjero en mi propio corazón. (*Vidente* 25)

> [Oh, God, defend my cause against those who wrote the texts of Genesis and Leviticus, of Romans, Corinthians and Timothy; or from those who, through their interpretation of such texts, crushed my hopes and condemned me to be a stranger in my own heart.]

Though it is ostensibly the "word of God" that alienates gays, heterosexism for Roig is not inherent in Christianity but in the vocabulary and traditional exegesis of certain Judeo-Christian scriptures. The "word of God," as incarnated in Christ, is for Roig the inspiration of the gay writer/rebel. He equates the gay male, whom he regards as a social pariah,[7] not only with the Carmelite mystics who informed his religious worldview but also with Christ himself because he was rejected by humanity and abandoned. It is through the figure of Christ that Roig in fact claims to find the encouragement necessary for resisting the heterosexism of both church and society: "Jesús me dará fuerza para empujar la rueda. Jesús está de parte de los homosexuales" (*Variaciones* 222) [Jesus will give me the strength to push the wheel. Jesus is on the side of homosexuals].

The language of "Mother Church," like that of Roig's biological mother, fails to grasp his inherent dignity as a gay man. It is ultimately negative, imposing on him the hypocrisy of either heterosexuality or chastity while concomitantly denying what is most uniquely human: freedom. Although Roig seeks to validate gayness, he comes to posit freedom as his ultimate goal. This is his universalization of the project of gay liberation.

Mi defensa de la homosexualidad es sólo el rostro concreto que toma mi defensa de la libertad. Y que en mi alegato contra las cadenas que oprimen a los homosexuales late una repulsa contra las estructuras que limitan al individuo. Todo lo demás es secundario. (*Vidente* 127)

[My defense of homosexuality is only the concrete face that my defense of freedom takes. And in my denunciation of the chains that oppress homosexuals pulsates a rejection of the structures that limit the individual. All the rest is secondary.]

To express the truth of human freedom, Roig announces the need for a new language "ajeno a tantas contradicciones y que partiese de una concepción más optimista del hombre" (*Variaciones* 223) [indifferent to so many contradictions and that would start with a more optimistic conception of man]. Through this new language Roig hopes to overcome the oppositions of hetero-relationality. Yet the indifference to contradiction that he envisions differs from that of homo-relationality insofar as it is to occur not within the prevailing discursive patterns that constitute its condition but outside, in a realm of impossible transcendence. Roig attempts to accede to this realm, but in the process leaves intact the real structures of his alienation as a gay man. Freedom as he conceives of it is thus an ideal rather than a reworking of the real.

It is in the context of this vision of freedom that Roig nonetheless propounds his concrete social agenda. Despite his overarching idealism, his words can be taken as the rallying cry of the entire gay movement of the post-Francoist and post-Stonewall era:

Gente avergonzada, en vez de languidecer junto a una letrina empuñad una pancarta, dirigíos al pulmón de la ciudad y allí gritad, gritad, gritad. Cuando se os acabe la voz haced huelga de hambre. Y, si es preciso, dejaos morir. Persistid en vuestra demanda hasta que os hagan justicia. Si se ríen de vosotros, no bajéis la mirada; si os hacen burla, herguíos hasta el cielo; si os combaten, dejaos matar. Preparad con sangre un mundo más honrado. Que más vale terminar los días en el surco, gritando, que pudrirse entre orines. (*Variaciones* 22)

[Shamed people, instead of languishing next to a latrine, take up a placard, head for the heart of the city and once there shout, shout, shout. When your voice gives out, go on a hunger strike. And, if it be necessary, let yourselves die. Persist in your demand until they do you justice. If they laugh at you, don't lower your gaze; if they make fun of you, raise your heads to the sky; if they fight you, let yourselves be killed. Prepare with blood a more honorable world. Better to end your days in the trenches, shouting, than rotting in urine.]

Roig responds to his own call to action not only through the act of writing but also through a sit-in that he stages in front of the convent after his expulsion and through public addresses. Nevertheless, the positive thrust of his appeal remains tied to standards of sexual morality that, according to certain members of the Spanish gay community, run counter to the project of gay liberation as a revolution of traditional sexual mores.[8]

Roig contends that gay men have historically been forced to express their sexuality in marginalized public spaces, such as parks and rest rooms, and in reflecting on the sexual dimension of the public/private dichotomy, he interprets the "letrina" as the contrary of the matrimonial bed. Whereas the latter, in keeping with the heterosexual ideology of the church, is the site of a life-giving and procreative sacrament, the former functions to equate gay sexuality with refuse and to reduce the gay male to the status of excrement. Roig does not speculate on the subversive potential of the marginal position of gays, and while Bersani in his analysis of Jean Genet suggests that only what society throws off can serve the future ("the paradoxical promise of fertility and renewal that Genet associates with waste" [180]), Roig, like many current activists, instructs gays to assume the same position as straights in order to achieve their privileges and power. Yet it is not clear how the attendant hierarchical oppressions of straight society will be avoided.

The Seer as Oracle

Despite his initial assertion of gay sexuality, Roig resists the label "homosexual" ascribed to him after the publication of *Parques*. He finds his freedom constrained by the term, and as a homosexual he discovers that his identity continues to be controlled by others. He declares that he has never been able to define himself and that he and all gays "terminan por ser tal como se les representa. Acaban por ser los pervertidos que la sociedad y la Iglesia deciden que sean" (*Vidente* 148) [end up being as they are represented. They end up being the perverts that society and the church decide that they are]. Through this decisive statement Roig abandons his effort to elucidate through autobiography an authentic gay voice for himself and those gay men who have none. More important, he expresses shame over his sexuality, and in so doing actually reverses the affirmative objective of the traditional coming-out narrative: "Cuando me di cuenta de que me había convertido en «el carmelita homosexual», «el cura homosexual», tuve asco de mí" (127) [When I realized that I had become the "homosexual Carmelite," "the homosexual priest," I was disgusted with myself]. This disgust is in fact the beginning of his final defeat.

Roig is utterly disappointed that *Parques* elicits only a lukewarm response from the Spanish gay community. As a result, he determines that though gays have been historically mistreated and maligned by society, they are too shallow to reflect on their exploitation, much less to seek solutions to it. In an effort to come to grips with his disillusion he constructs a dialogue between himself and what he imagines to be the archetypal, collective gay voice. This is the voice promised from the outset of his autobiographical project and so anxiously awaited by the reader.

The gay voice that speaks, like the one haunting the vision of Lorca in "Oda a Walt Whitman," informs him that its nature is inconstant, unstable, and lascivious:

> Quieres sacarnos a plena luz cuando en realidad la gente, a plena luz, se aburre. Nosotros no conocemos el aburrimiento porque hoy destruimos lo que edificamos ayer, hoy odiamos lo que anoche besamos y acariciamos lo que mañana arrojaremos desdeñosamente en un rincón. Nuestra naturaleza, aunque te empeñes en pensar lo contrario, es promiscua. (*Vidente* 171)

> [You want to draw us into the broad daylight when in reality people in broad daylight are bored. We do not know boredom because we destroy today what we constructed yesterday, we hate today what last night we kissed, and we caress what tomorrow we will throw away with disdain in a corner. Our nature, even though you insist on thinking the contrary, is promiscuous.]

Roig erred in his attempt to place gay love within the framework of Christian matrimony. As his interlocutor tells him, the gay male is antimonogamous. His sole pleasure consists in corrupting youthful innocence, and his only fear is that with age he will be unable to sustain his sexual profligacy. Whereas Roig once saw in the "gay pariah" the drama of Christian martyr-dom, he now discovers in him a small and narrow world: "Nuestra soledad está hecha a la medida de nuestra vida: pequeña, insignificante, rastrera" (172) [Our solitude is made to the measurement of our lives: small, insig-nificant, contemptible]. Finally, then, the gay essence is both degenerate and banal. As such, it serves as the preeminent sign of contrariety through which the value of hetero-normativity is constituted.

Throughout this extended dialogue, the gay speaker has no concrete identity, but in the end Roig discloses that its voice is his: "El hombrecillo homosexual, insignificante y cínico, que ha construido un amor a la medida de su incapacidad soy yo" (174) [I am the little homosexual man, insignifi-cant and cynical, who built a love to the measurement of his incapacity]. Through the autobiographical undertaking Roig hoped to destroy this "hombrecillo despreciable" (174) [despicable little man] and realize a new identity. He was unable to do so, however, because the voice of the hetero-sexual other had anchored itself permanently within him, defining him in alterity and relentlessly ventriloquizing his own voice. His life writing is hence heterobiographical in that it is constructed through a fundamental self/other binary and also in the more narrow sense that it simply transcribes the gay life as dictated to the homosexual life writer by the heterosexual other. Though as a gay Christian Roig prophesies a coming out from dark-ness into light, anticipating the death of the old man and the birth of the new, he remains inextricably bound to the past, and the "new" voice that he enunciates is in reality the same old voice of heterosexist oppression.[9] The upshot, to cite the words of Michael Sprinker, is that "the self is constituted by a discourse that it never completely masters" (342).

Rather than challenge the voice of homosexuality that he hears, Roig ac-cepts it as his own. As a consequence, the process of alienation is all but com-plete, and the sought-after voice of gay autonomy is finally reabsorbed within the dominant voice of hetero-relationality. Roig's recognition of this state of affairs, however, is itself a kind of rebellion, but in this moment re-bellion, blind and absurd, is unable to articulate itself in a way that might effect positive change in the world. When Roig dreams of being asked to re-tract all that he has written, "la única palabra que fui capaz de pronunciar fue: — ¡Mierda!" (*Vidente* 181) [the only word that I was capable of pronouncing was "shit!"]. This, then, is the suffocated voice of authenticity that affirms itself ultimately only in the imaginary, but that affirms itself nonetheless.

Roig comes to acknowledge that his entire life writing is undermined by his apologetic impulse: "desde el momento que trato de justificarme ya me confieso culpable" (*Vidente* 137) [from the moment that I try to justify myself I already confess myself guilty]. As a confession, his autobiography asserts gay identity in terms of a discourse intended to condemn it, and though he imagines a language capable of transmitting the voice of an autonomous and unified gay self, he concludes that "las palabras nacen muertas entre mis dedos" (*Vidente* 166) [words are born dead within my fingers].[10] This final vision of a stillborn language is significant, for while it recognizes the limitations of autobiographical prosopopeia, it neither dispels the notion of an extralinguistic self nor allows for a dislodging of heterorelationality. Instead, it ossifies language, and in so doing freezes gay identity as a negative essence. Roig thus remains enchanted to the end by a belief in the duality of the self and language and of the power of the latter to alienate.

Roig is subverted not only through the confessional mode of autobiographical discourse but also through his more general effort to achieve a positive gay identity within the institution of the church. Throughout the seventies and eighties dramatic change has occurred in the lives of Spanish lesbians and gay men. It has taken place, however, largely in spite of the church, which continues to turn a deaf ear to the demands of gay men and lesbians for the full recognition of their civil and human rights. For this reason the personal failure of Roig can be viewed as part of the church's refusal to participate and assist in the construction of a more humane and just society. Roig's case is particularly ironic since only in the hostile environment of the church was he motivated enough to defend gay sexuality. As he gradually became separated from the church, his disillusion with the project of gay liberation increased, and while at the end of the dictatorship in 1975 he was prepared to lay down his life for the realization of his ideals, by the time of his expulsion from the priesthood, he had reached the bitter conclusion that nothing on earth was worth such a struggle (*Vidente* 165).

Notwithstanding the failure of Roig's written word, there are small moments of triumph in his life as recounted in the autobiographical texts.

Once, for example, he is hounded by a man in a Valencia park who, like the one that provoked his arrest in London, attempts to blackmail him. Roig manages to extricate himself from the clutches of his tormenter, only to encounter him years later in the same park. Yet rather than avoid him, he chooses on this occasion to face him and to make him feel shame for his harassment of gays. Afterward, he expresses a kind of gay pride for not having fled:

Cuando quedó detrás de mí me sentí dichoso. Mi vida puede ser un fracaso. Otros compañeros de sacerdocio pueden haber ascendido cumbres de renombre. Puedo haber quedado marcado para el resto de mis días. Pero sólo por un momento como ése, sólo por haber sido capaz de mirar fijamente a un opresor de homosexuales y haberle obligado a bajar la mirada, a descontrolarse y a balbucir nerviosamente un saludo servil, doy por bien empleados todos los caminos de soledad que he recorrido. (*Variaciones* 186)

[When he was behind me I felt fortunate. My life might be a failure. Other colleagues in the priesthood might have risen to heights of fame. I might have been marked for the rest of my days. But only for a moment like that, only for having been capable of looking straight at an oppressor of homosexuals and having forced him to lower his gaze, to lose his composure and nervously stammer a servile greeting, I consider worthwhile all the paths of solitude that I have traveled.]

In this instance gay pride is an act performed, not in reciprocity with other gay men or lesbians, but in opposition to an oppressor of gays — though one might argue that this hustler, like Roig's mother, is himself a victim of societal oppression. What is significant is that Roig no longer seeks refuge in the ostensibly private sphere of hetero-normativity nor through recourse to an ideal self beyond the structures of hetero-relationality, but on the very site of his own oppression. It is here, then, that gay autobiography actually begins to work and that the changes so ardently desired by Roig might in fact be set in motion.

Juan Goytisolo

Cutting the Gordian Knot

Goytisolo advances an anti-essentialist conception of the self through-out most of his writings,[1] but in his explicitly autobiographical texts, *Coto vedado* [*Forbidden Territory*] and *En los reinos de taifa* [*Realms of Strife*], he attempts to inscribe an inherently gay identity, recounting his alienation as a gay man while struggling to release his voice from the discursive constraints through which it has been repressed and silenced. In contrast to Roig, who dreamed of transcending the discourse of heterosexism only to discover in his own voice the echo of his heterosexual oppressors, Goytisolo works within a hetero-relational discourse so as not to normalize homosexuality but instead to continue the systematic and relentless attack on dominant cultural and sexual norms launched in the midsixties with his "trilogy of treason."[2] His life writing is thus heterobiographical in that he positions his gay self in opposition to a hetero-oriented society. Moreover, he maintains a rigorous self/other dichotomy in the narration of his sexual relationships with other men. Goytisolo is keenly aware of the exploitation of gay men and lesbians, and unlike Roig, he is alert to his own complicity in the heterosexual regime. But it is only in his more recent fictional writing, rather than in the autobiographies themselves, that he comes to integrate himself into a common gay struggle and begins to delineate the trajectory of homo-relationality.

Within the overall chronology of the autobiographies, the titles of the two volumes suggest that the self of the past is inaccessible and that the self of the present is psychically splintered and riven with turmoil. Yet the two meta-phors are temporally and egologically coextensive, and while the forbidden territory indicates the elusive gay self, the realms of strife represent the sites of conflict with the various oppressive identities (including those of Catholic, Castilian, Spanish, European, white, and bourgeois) superimposed on Goy-tisolo from the outset of his life. In the autobiographies, nevertheless, the preeminent alien identity is that of the heterosexual, and on the most funda-mental plane the psychic life of the autobiographical persona is dichotomous in structure and characterized not by a multiplicity of selves but by two: the homosexual and the heterosexual, or the real and the fake. The heterosexual is depicted as inhabiting the homosexual like an unwanted guest who usurps his voice and converts him into a ventriloquist (*Coto vedado* 40; hereafter *CV*). Goytisolo undertakes the autobiographical enterprise precisely in or-der to exorcise this intruder and sever once and for all the Gordian knot (*En los reinos de taifa* 217; hereafter *RT*) of hetero-relationality that binds his ho-moerotic desire and gags his authentic gay voice.

As autobiographer Goytisolo seeks to inscribe a gay identity and at the same time save himself and his entire past from oblivion and nothingness. He thus speculates on life writing as an instrument of ontologization, and following a near-fatal accident he reveals an

> urgencia y necesidad de escribir, expresarte, no permitir que cuanto amas, tu pasado, experiencia, emociones, lo que eres y has sido desaparezcan contigo, resolución de luchar con uñas y dientes contra el olvido. (*CV* 29)

> [urgency and need to write, express yourself, not to allow all that you love, your past experience, emotions, what you are and have been, to disappear with you, determination to fight tooth and claw against oblivion. (*Forbidden Territory* 21; hereafter *FT*)]

This desire for the permanence of the written word lies at the heart of tradi-tional autobiography as a project of egological recovery and essentializa-tion.[3] Like a traditional autobiographer Goytisolo aims to reconstruct his past as accurately and honestly as possible. At times he seems anxious to maintain a strict chronological order, correcting himself for inadvertently straying from the story line (*RT* 15) and informing the reader when he intentionally interrupts the temporal succession of events (*RT* 138, 144).[4] What is more, he is wont to employ the analytical method of a historian, consulting old papers and letters and making notations whenever necessary to confirm hypotheses and conjectures. Letters comprise significant portions of the two texts, and it is through a letter to his companion, Monique, reproduced in *En los reinos de taifa,* that he first acknowledges in writing that he is gay: "total, definitiva, irremediablemente homosexual" (240) ["totally, definitively, irrevocably homosexual" (*Realms of Strife* 204; hereafter *RS*)]. This private disclosure is made public and "confessed" in the autobiographies. In fact the entire life writing of Goytisolo is endowed with a quasi-confessional quality, and like Roig he wonders if it might in reality serve as a lay substitute for the sacrament of confession (*CV* 40). In keeping with the confessional tradition, Goytisolo vows to be rigorously sincere and uncompromising in his self-examination, and promises to reveal "lo más duro y difícil de expresar, lo que no has dicho todavía a nadie, recuerdo odiosamente vil o humillante, el trago más amargo de tu vida" (*CV* 41) ["what is most painful and difficult to express, what you haven't yet said to anybody, an odiously vile or humiliating memory, the bitterest blow in your life" (*FT* 32)].

As is typical of lesbian and gay life writers, Goytisolo conceives of gay identity as existing both potentially and in actuality. He expresses his relation to this "yo genuino" (*CV* 139) ["real . . . self" (*FT* 116)] in part through the pronominal structure of the texts, narrating his past life largely in first person while occasionally employing third person when the self of the past eludes him. Yet the principal first-person, past-tense narrative is repeatedly punctuated by a multitensed second-person narrative. (In *Coto vedado* the second-person narrative is often in italic, although changes in the typeface, especially in *En los reinos de taifa,* do not necessarily correspond to a change in voice.) Through the second person, Goytisolo addresses himself in the moment of writing, and in so doing strives to articulate the existence that has been denied him. His autobiography is therefore both a reflection on a past life, albeit a life that was not so much his own as that of the heterosexual other within him, as well as an effort to realize a new life in the present and for the future. The opposing discourses of the autobiographical texts in fact intersect throughout much of the writing of Goytisolo. James D. Fernández equates his more "legible" discourse with heterosexual normativity ("La novela familiar del autobiógrafo" 59). Annie Perrin, moreover, actually discerns a confrontation between what she calls "heterotextuality," or a linear discourse intended to reproduce reality, and "homotextuality," which she defines as a writing of deviance founded on a notion of a self-engendering and autonomous text that subverts traditional narrative paradigms and the norms that they support (75). In the autobiographies this homotextuality is most thoroughly developed in the second-person sections.

Whereas Roig attempts to grasp an authentic gay voice through a revindication of the father figure and a concomitant destruction of the mother, Goytisolo seeks to release his voice through an extended gesture of discursive parricide.[5] Unlike the early years of Roig, Goytisolo's childhood during the Spanish Civil War was marked by a series of violent events that disrupted his family life and led to the death of his mother in a Nationalist bombing raid over Barcelona. Though he explicitly identifies himself as the offspring of the violence of the war itself (*CV* 66), the death of his mother comes to signify for him retrospectively the origin of his own cultural and sexual exile. She was an intellectual and a liberal, and her family was prominent in the Catalán resurgence at the turn of the twentieth century. What is more, it is among her relatives and ancestors that Goytisolo discovers gay sexuality. His paternal family, in contrast, descended from Cuban slaveowners, and unlike his mother, his father was pro-fascist, pro-Castilian, pro-Catholic, and virulently heterosexist. To a certain degree, Goytisolo endeavors to purge this anti-gay father figure and recreate the lost and silenced world of the mother as he imagines it to have been.[6] He therefore differs not only from Roig but also from a whole tradition of male life writers who take as their point of departure the search for an ideal or missing father.

In the course of time, Goytisolo comes to regard Franco, rather than his biological father, as the capstone in the edifice of heterosexual patriarchy, and it is against him that he directs his discursive attacks. He describes the dictator as "ese otro Padre castrador y tiránico" (*CV* 250) ["that other tyrannical, castrating Father" (*FT* 212)] and reveals that his hatred for him developed into a veritable obsession (*CV* 250). What is ironic is that after rejecting the politics of the father and immersing himself in communism through extensive visits to the Soviet Union and Cuba, Goytisolo experiences the same heterosexism of his youth under Francoism and Catholicism. He is made acutely aware of this contradiction while interviewing Che Guevara during a visit to Cuba in the early sixties. On a table next to Guevara is a book by the gay Cuban writer Virgilio Piñera. When Guevara notices the book, he exclaims: "Quién coño lee aquí a ese maricón?" (*RT* 175) ["Who the fuck's reading that pansy?" (*RS* 147)]. This episode provokes in Goytisolo a feeling of deep solidarity with the gay victims of Castro and is part of his own slow and excruciating process of coming out.

The decisive moment in Goytisolo's coming out in fact occurs in Cuba during a rally at a communist youth camp. The camp directors had recently expelled two lesbian girls, and as Goytisolo participates in the rally he realizes his duplicity in the context of Castroite politics and his profound alienation as a gay man in a heterosexist society. He begins to recite a litany of epithets intended to denounce the false heterosexual self that inhabits him: "fantasma," "zombi," "fantoche," "autómata," "pelele," "impostor," "simulador," "enemigo," and "otro" (*CV* 139) ["ghost," "zombie," "puppet," "robot," "rag doll," "impostor," "pretender," "enemy," and "other" (*FT* 116–17)]. In the process he is overcome by "un brusco e imperioso afán de autenticidad" (*CV* 140) ["a sudden, overpowering desire for authenticity" (*FT* 117)] and determines that he must silence the voice that has ceased to represent him so that he can represent his oppressors (*CV* 139) and ungag and rescue his own voice (*CV* 139). This *prise de conscience* marks a turning point in his life and the beginning of a new phase in his writing that will culminate in the autobiographical project itself.

For Goytisolo, nonetheless, the self is internally mediated by alterity, and though he pursues authenticity, he is doubtful from the outset of ever achieving his goal. While still narrating the events of his early childhood, he interjects the case of a prisoner of Francoism whose psychic as well as physical space had been constituted as a jail from which escape was inconceivable even in the imaginary:

> La prisión se había infiltrado en su fuero interno sin autorizarle escapatoria alguna. Las muchachas que había conocido en su juventud, heroínas de su libido nocturna, actuaban siempre en una escena penitenciaria. El castigo impuesto por el tribunal militar conseguía así, al cabo de los años, la victoria absoluta: encierro no sólo físico, sino asimismo quimérico, imaginario, mental. (*CV* 84)

[The prison had penetrated his inner being and allowed him no escape whatsoever. The girls he had known in his youth, heroines of his nocturnal libido, always performed in a prison setting. The military tribunal's punishment thus won after many years an absolute victory: not only a prison for the body, but likewise for mind, imagination, and fantasy. (*FT* 69)]

This prison functions like the Panopticon of Jeremy Bentham, the model penitentiary of Enlightenment reform that according to Foucault in *Discipline and Punish* became the paradigm for social and psychological policing in the modern capitalist state. In the Panopticon the prisoners can all be seen at the same time from a central watchtower, and since they are never certain if they are being observed, they begin to monitor their every action, ultimately becoming the agents of their own incarceration and enslavement. For Goytisolo this is the situation of both the prisoner of Francoism and the repressed homosexual within the heterosexual hegemony. Like the inhabitants of the Panopticon, gays are unable to "come out" of the prison world of their closet to the extent that they have internalized what they perceive as an all-seeing heterosexual eye whose look regulates their behavior from within. In the life recounted in *Coto vedado* and *En los reinos de taifa* this look, emanating from the male heterosexual other, represents the dynamic of hetero-relationality that alienates gays and that Goytisolo, in spite of the odds, attempts through writing to resist.[7]

The Straight Look

With regard to his sexual development, the most significant family member in Goytisolo's life is his gay maternal grandfather, Ricardo. In what is doubtlessly for first-time readers the most startling passage of the entire autobiographical narrative, Goytisolo describes how his grandfather repeatedly molests him as a child one summer.[8] The young Juan reveals his ordeal to his brother José Agustín, whom he swears to secrecy, but the latter informs their father, and as a result both grandfather and grandmother are driven from the house and forced to take up residence elsewhere. The enormity of the situation is made manifest through "la mirada justiciera y reprobadora del yerno" (*CV* 103) ["the righteous, reproving gaze of their son-in-law" (*FT* 86)]. Afterward, the grandparents continue to take their meals in the family house and Ricardo provides them with financial support over the years, but from Goytisolo's adult perspective the money is exacted by his father through a kind of blackmail. The father in fact uses the grandfather not only to replenish his pocketbook but also to reaffirm his masculine, heterosexual identity and to foster his moral superiority. Through the negative dynamics of hetero-relationality, the lives of the two men eventually become locked in a sado-masochistic struggle that is resolved only through their almost simultaneous deaths.

Though Goytisolo does not attempt to exonerate his grandfather, he feels a deep compassion for him, pitying his inability to react positively to his condition as a gay man and empathizing with the suffering that he endures over the years in his relationship with his son-in-law. According to Goytisolo, Ricardo internalizes the heterosexist ideology of his culture and comes to envision his sexuality as a personal tragedy and a curse. Like the prisoner of the Panopticon, and indeed like Roig at the end of *Vidente en rebeldía,* he functions as his own worst judge and shortly before dying bemoans homosexual passion as a hateful sin that offends God and ruined his whole life. For Goytisolo this is a declaration of moral cowardice and an admission of defeat, and it is precisely to avoid such a fate that he chooses to affirm his own sexuality and ultimately to write his autobiography:[9]

> El recuerdo de este automenosprecio consecutivo al desdén de los demás, de este oprobio asumido y transmutado en culpabilidad interna pesó muy fuerte en la decisión de afirmar mi destino contra viento y marea, de poner las cosas en claro frente al prójimo y a mí mismo. (*CV* 105)

> [The memory of this self-contempt resulting from the scorn of others, of the shame that was accepted and transmuted into inner guilt, weighed very heavily in my decision to affirm my destiny whatever the cost, and to set everything out clearly for myself and others. (*FT* 87)]

Goytisolo thus seeks to overcome the negatively constituted essence of gay male sexuality. What is ironic is that his reading of the grandfather comes close to replicating that very essence to the extent that it blurs the distinction between gay sexuality and child molestation. Ricardo is the victim of heterosexism, both in the home and in the public sphere, where he is arrested for his sexual conduct. But he is also a perpetrator of abuse.

Although Goytisolo rejects his heterosexual father and his homosexual grandfather, he is attracted as a small boy to a working-class and presumably straight man named Jaume, whose job is to escort the father to his factory during the revolutionary period in Barcelona at the beginning of the Spanish Civil War. Goytisolo indicates that despite his young age he is in love with Jaume, who is kind and patient with children and tolerant of the views and beliefs of others. What particularly fascinates him, however, is the revolver that Jaume carries to protect the father. In the eyes of the child, the revolver endows Jaume with a larger-than-life stature. Yet it is a weapon of violence and its presence is an indication and a consequence of war. Moreover, though it intrigues the child, it stands between him and his friend, mediating their experience and revealing the societal violence that plagues male sociality. This violence in fact appears, albeit in mitigated form, in several of Goytisolo's relationships with his peers. Once, for example, he feels compelled to spit and urinate on the house of a hydrocephalic child, while in school he is at times the object of abuse by the other boys. On another occasion, he and his brother Luis engage in an act of wanton destruction by hacking at a heap of old family furniture. From his adult perspective this action is particularly significant insofar as it is motivated by "el ansia informulada, secreta de hacer escuchar su voz" (*CV* 67) ["the unconscious, secret desire to make their voices heard" (*FT* 55)]. As a writer Goytisolo will strive to turn the gratuitous and random violence of his childhood back against the culture that produced it. But in so doing he will inadvertently maintain the structures of hetero-relationality through which violence operates.

Goytisolo's homosocial and homosexual experiences in later youth and early adulthood take place in an explicitly hetero-relational framework. During his university period in Madrid, he is drawn to a fellow student named Lucho. Lucho is somewhat older than Goytisolo and frequently in the company of an overly possessive and jealous companion. Lucho and Goytisolo nevertheless begin to spend evenings together drinking in student taverns. Once, while thoroughly intoxicated, they embrace, and Goytisolo caresses Lucho "bajo la mirada impasible del camarero" (*CV* 186) ["under the waiter's impassive gaze" (*FT* 158)]. The next day, after the waiter informs all of their friends of the incident, Goytisolo feels as if his behavior had been completely involuntary and wonders if some secret "Mr. Hyde" within had taken advantage of his drunkenness and acted according to his own intentions. This alienation of his spontaneous homoerotic desire is effected most immediately through the look of the waiter, which, in keeping with the heterosexual ideology that it represents, exposes his sexuality while shaming him into a denial that leads to what elsewhere he describes as a sensation of schizophrenia (*CV* 139).

The mechanism of this look becomes even more apparent in Lucho himself. Lucho does not condemn Goytisolo for what has happened but rather takes him to two prostitutes, Mely and Fernandita. The songs they sing together set the stage for what transpires that evening and continue to haunt Goytisolo's subsequent relationships with men for years to come: "*Mira que están mirando / que nos miramos*" (*CV* 188) ["Look they are looking at us looking at each other" (*FT* 160)]. Lucho, like the dominant male, sits with Mely and Fernandita on his knees while watching the lesser Goytisolo on the sidelines: "con sus ojos negros, metálicos, insondables y duros como la mica, me observaba a mí" (*CV* 189) ["(he) observed me with his dark, metallic, inscrutable eyes as hard as mica" (*FT* 160)]. This unidirectional look invades Goytisolo, appropriating his sexual desire and hetero-izing it. Yet the process of hetero-ization is carried out not by Lucho but by Goytisolo himself, "Yo interpreté aquello como una orden silenciosa" (*CV* 189) ["I interpreted this as a silent (message)" (*FT* 160)], as well as by Mely, who assumes the heterosexual look while remaining the object of the overarching look of Lucho. Goytisolo and Mely in reality occupy the same side of the sexual divide, since unlike the unfathomable and hostile eyes of Lucho, Mely's are "claros y hermosos" (*CV* 189) ["beautiful and clear" (*FT* 160)] and hence themselves susceptible to observation. Through the presence of Lucho her look is momentarily transformed into an act of physical penetration: "me separó los labios con los suyos e introdujo entre ellos, como un dardo, su lengua" (*CV* 189) ["her lips separated mine and her . . . tongue entered my mouth like a dart" (*FT* 160)]. Finally, however, Mely is not the agent of seduction but the instrument of Lucho, whose ostensible aim is not to unite with Goytisolo in a subliminal homoerotic bond but to produce in him a masculine sameness through his own eventual act of penetration:

Lucho había sacado entre tanto los pechos a Fernandita, pero advertí que vigilaba mis progresos con el rabillo del ojo. Su aprobación implícita y mi ansiedad por abolir la memoria de mi pasada conducta, me animaron a seguir su ejemplo. (*CV* 189)

[Meanwhile Lucho had taken Fernandita's breasts but I noticed that he was following my progress out of the corner of his eye. His implicit approval and my desire to eradicate all memory of my past behavior encouraged me to copy his example. (*FT* 160–61)]

When the whole episode is over, Goytisolo reveals a "sensación de alivio, de haber lavado la mancha, de ser como los demás, de poder mirar otra vez de cara, sin sonrojarme, a Lucho y sus amigos" (*CV* 189) ["feeling of relief at washing away the stain, . . . (of being) the same as everybody else, . . . (of being able to) look Lucho and his friends in the face without blushing" (*FT* 161)]. In this way Goytisolo is reinstated, albeit precariously, into the tribe of straight men. He will no longer be the object of their look but will temporarily adopt the male heterosexual look and direct it toward women. The experience with Mely thus marks the beginning of his adventures with prostitutes.[10]

Mely, Fernandita, and Goytisolo are all manipulated by Lucho. But the latter is the most ironic of the foursome since he feels obligated to take on the role of policing his and Goytisolo's sexuality, quelling their fleeting (and mutual) sexual attraction while reducing the two women to the status of objects. Later, in a drunken stupor, Lucho invites Goytisolo to lie next to him on his bed, perhaps, as Goytisolo fears, to test him further. Now, however, a heterosexual "they," like the "public" of Lorca's lovers, has moved from the exterior world of the tavern and ensconced itself in the seemingly private sphere of the bedroom — "look they are looking at us looking at each other." Goytisolo therefore leaves the room, and for the moment, at least, "Mr. Hyde no reapareció" (*CV* 192) ["Mr. Hyde did not reappear" (163 *FT*)]. Goytisolo hence remains a "homonym" (*CV* 150) and as such caught in a state of alterity. His homoeroticism is effectively repressed, and an incipient homo-relationality is hetero-ized and dispersed.

At the end of *Coto vedado* Goytisolo describes a relationship with another male, Raimundo. A heterosexual possibly of gypsy background, Raimundo is a marginal figure who lives and sleeps in the area along the Barcelona port. Goytisolo is attracted to him physically, but as he later realizes, his passion is kindled specifically by the exoticism and otherness that he attributes to Raimundo.

> El abismo cultural y social existente entre vosotros cumple, cumplirá en lo futuro, ese papel diferencial, de aproximación fascinada a lo desconocido y ajeno que corresponde usualmente a la disimilitud complementaria de los dos sexos. (*CV* 224)

> [The social, cultural abyss existing between you fulfills, will fulfill in the future, that differentiating role, fascinating closeness to what is alien and unknown usually corresponding to the complementary dissimilarity between the two sexes. (*FT* 190)]

This is a key passage (whose theme is repeated elsewhere in the autobiographies), for in it Goytisolo begins to transfer the self/other binary of hetero-relationality (the complementary but nonetheless hierarchized dissimilarity of the two sexes) to homosocial and homosexual intercourse. The sexual imaginary that Goytisolo fabricates is thus, strictly speaking, not homo-erotic but heteroerotic insofar as difference, rather than sameness, constitutes its condition and determines the trajectory of its expression. Despite that, his ostensible aim will not be to enforce difference but rather to bridge the social and cultural divide between himself and what he perceives to be the historically oppressed other, first detected in Raimundo and later in his Muslim lovers.

Raimundo and Goytisolo meet in a floating bar at the edge of the Barcelona dockyards. This frontier zone, between the hetero-ized world of the city and the amorphousness of the sea, draws a variety of marginal persons and seems a propitious site for the expression of the young Juan's desire. As with Lucho, he and Raimundo are observed by an ever-watchful proprietor. In the absence of overt homoeroticism (Raimundo is completely oblivious to the silent longing of his companion) this straight look is for all intents and purposes benign. Yet given the radical subject position of heterosexual masculinity, its meaning remains unknowable: "los dos bebéis coñac y cerveza en un rincón bajo la búdica, impenetrable mirada del dueño" (*CV* 224) ["you both drink beer and cognac in one corner beneath the owner's impenetrable, Buddha gaze" (*FT* 190)]. On one occasion, Goytisolo contrives to spend the night with Raimundo in his hovel, but their relationship is never consummated. While here, Goytisolo feels powerless to enunciate what from his perspective is "una pasión imposible y sin nombre" (*CV* 226) ["an impossible, nameless passion" (*FT* 191)] precisely because of the overwhelming name already inscribed within the heterosexist discourse that he fears the straight Raimundo will invoke if he approaches him physically: "el término infame de maricón" (*CV* 226) ["the vile term 'queer' " (*FT* 191)]. Afterward, Goytisolo continues to visit Raimundo, and once they join a prostitute who, like Mely, mediates their relationship: "pasearéis los tres del brazo, con la mujer pintada y obesa entre ambos" (*CV* 227) ["you, all three, walk along hand in hand, with the obese, painted woman in between" (*FT* 192)]. With the passage of time, however, Goytisolo is even further distanced from Raimundo, and, unable to unite with him, he eventually comes to regard him as material for his future writing. The subject/object dichotomy that he experiences vis-à-vis this masculine, lower-class figure will in fact repeat itself throughout his subsequent, sexual relationships with Muslim men.

In the Sotadic Zone

In *En los reinos de taifa* Goytisolo describes his first intimate relationship with a Muslim, Mohamed, and his initiation into the Islamic world that eventually dominates his later life. Having experienced the plight of a gay man in a heterosexist society, he considers himself sensitive to the alienation of the non-European minorities living in his midst in Paris, the site of his own self-exile from Spain. He chooses to identify with them, but as a European he at first perceives their world as an inaccessible and forbidden territory: "Ningún europeo penetraba en él, como si una frontera invisible se lo vedara" (*RT* 223) ["No European ever set foot there, as if an invisible frontier forbade entry" (*RS* 189)]. The look of its inhabitants, moreover, is elusive and perhaps even mocking of his tentative efforts to enter within: "¿con qué ojos podían mirar a un *nesrani* que con timidez pretendía asomarse a su gueto?" (*RT* 224) ["how would they look upon a *nesrani* who nervously peered into their ghetto?" (*RS* 190)]. Through Mohamed, nevertheless, Goytisolo begins to traverse the cultural gap.

Goytisolo meets Mohamed in a café (where the waiter seems indifferent to their presence), and the latter asks him for a light. When Goytisolo, whose hands are trembling, gives him a match, Mohamed responds in a mestizo language, mixing Arabic and French ("*Merci, juya*" [*RT* 224]) and thereby delineating a linguistic and cultural border zone of interaction, halfway, as it were, between Africa and Europe, Islam and Christianity. The result is a short-lived but intense sexual relationship. Afterward, Goytisolo takes on a study of the Arabic language, as well as a series of Muslim lovers, motivated by "una porfiada voluntad de acercamiento a un modelo físico y cultural de cuerpo cuyo fulgor e incandescencia me guiaban como un faro" (*RT* 225) ["(a) resolution to draw nearer to a physical and cultural bodily ideal, the white heat and refulgence of which guided me like a beacon" (*RS* 191)]. Though the pursuit of this ideal involves a rejection of the sexually, socially, and racially repressive culture of Goytisolo's Spanish and European background, it is the consequence of an a priori European exoticization of the Muslim. Classic European orientalism, according to Edward W. Said, conceives of the East as inherently feminine, and hence susceptible to penetration and possession by the West (44, 138); but as Joseph A. Boone points out, stereotypical colonialist images of the East include, among others, the "hypervirile Arab" (91). In constructing within Europe his own "Sotadic Zone" Goytisolo ascribes to his Muslim lovers this exotic, masculine identity already prefigured in Raimundo, through which he himself is physically objectified.[11] Yet "instinctively" (or, more precisely, through the overdeterminism of hetero-relationality), he responds to physical objectification by exerting over his sexual partners his own intellectual prowess: "poseído de ellos y su placer áspero, buscaba instintivamente la manera de contrapesar mi sumisión física con una dominación intelectual capaz de establecer el equilibrio entre los platillos de la balanza" (*RT* 228) ["possessed by them and their rough pleasure, I instinctively looked for a way to counterbalance my physical submission with an intellectual domination capable of establishing an equilibrium between both scales" (*RS* 193)]. This domination is achieved specifically through his knowledge of French and his ability to write letters, that is, through his voice.

Through letters the European Goytisolo gives voice to his Muslim lovers.[12] In so doing he comes to control them through the power of the word by negotiating their personal and business affairs. Once firmly in place, however, the subject/object dichotomy of his sexual relationships becomes tedious, and with regard to Mohamed, he writes: "Con un fatalismo que a veces me irritaba, Mohamed ponía su destino en mis manos; mas si ello le descargaba de toda responsabilidad tocante a su futuro, me abrumaba a mí con los deberes de una engorrosa tutoría moral" (*RT* 228) ["With a fatalism that often irritated me, Mohamed placed his destiny in my hands; but if that relieved him of all responsibility for his future, it burdened me with the duties of an irksome moral guardian" (*RS* 194)]. These relationships are transitory, but a pattern is established, and a model of Arabic masculinity becomes fixed in Goytisolo's erotic imaginary. Though as Paul Julian Smith indicates, he dares "not admit that his 'innate attraction' (p. 207) [*RT*] to working class, Arab men is based on a physical desire that hypostatizes 'race' as a fixed and essential identity" (*Laws* 38), he in fact partakes of what Tomás Almaguer has succinctly labeled "colonial desires" and "class-coded lust" (265).

At the end of *En los reinos de taifa,* after coming out to Monique, Goytisolo travels to Morocco for an extended stay and has an affair with an unnamed Moroccan man. He narrates the episode through a variety of pronominal voices, but increasingly employs the third person, as if the self of the past were continually slipping into heterogeneity. He thus writes: "El expatriado ha encontrado a un amigo" (*RT* 300) ["The expatriate has found a friend" (*RS* 253)]. Although of the same age as Goytisolo, this new friend is clearly of the working class, having spent fifteen years in the Tangier dockyards loading boats until he lost his job and became Goytisolo's companion. Just as Jaume guarded Goytisolo's father during the revolutionary period in Barcelona, the Moroccan protects Goytisolo on his excursions through the underworld of Tangier. In both instances there is a threat of violence, but while in Spain during the thirties it occurred against a backdrop of class exploitation, in Tangier it appears in a broadened context of class and ethnic antagonisms. (It is not only as a bourgeois but also as a European that Goytisolo might be attacked.) Jaume, moreover, was preempted from the working class by the bourgeois Goytisolos and made into their buffer against social disorder; the Moroccan, on the other hand, remains independent, and through him the violence that has haunted Goytisolo since early childhood at last erupts.

One night while drinking Goytisolo provokes a violent outburst on the part of his Moroccan friend. In so doing he seeks to effect a cathartic destruction of the alien identities that have burdened him throughout his life. As the Moroccan strikes Goytisolo in the face (it is specifically Goytisolo's eyes that are hit), he makes Goytisolo the object of his look: "se planta sin quitarte la vista de encima" (*RT* 303) ["(he) stands there not taking his eyes off you" (*RS* 256)]. Whereas on previous occasions the look emanated from the European male heterosexual, it now issues from a working-class Muslim whose sexual identity defies easy categorization within the conventional heterosexual/homosexual binarism of Western culture. Yet its function is ultimately identical: rather than reveal an authentic self (the homo) it produces the same "self-in-alterity" of hetero-relationality. Following the beating, Goytisolo experiences an "esfuerzo trabajoso de levantarse, ir al baño, mirarse con incredulidad en el espejo y descubrir un rostro que no es el tuyo" (*RT* 303) ["(a) painful effort to get up, go to the bathroom, look at oneself incredulously in the mirror and find a face that is not yours" (*RS* 256)]. For a moment he wobbles, both physically, in his shaken state, and discursively, through the jarring shift in persons ("mirarse" and "el tuyo"), and though he is finally at the threshold of authenticity, the ideal "yo genuino" continues to elude him.

The Moroccan subsequently pleads for a rapprochement, but Goytisolo rejects him: "tú quieres estar a solas, digerir lo acaecido, poner tierra por medio, transformar humillación en levadura, furia en apoderamiento" (*RT* 303) ["you want to be alone, to digest what has happened, distance yourself, transform humiliation into yeast, rage into power" (*RS* 256)]. Goytisolo's aim is to make of his ordeal a catalyst for artistic creation. As Smith explains, the "metaphorical fixing of identity soon cedes to a metonymic displacement. Experience will be transmuted into writing, the written body into the writing of the body (into homographesis)" (*Laws* 41). In this writing, born from an internalization of violence, Goytisolo attacks the culture that he so despises. He becomes a latter-day Don Julián, a victimized object turned avenging subject, taking a pen as his sword and language as his field of battle. The irony is that as "writer-warrior" he maintains the same subject/object dichotomy of hetero-relationality and remains detached from other gay men. The scope of this hetero-relationality is revealed precisely through the sado-masochistic sexual dynamic of the encounter with the Moroccan.

It might seem, when the European Goytisolo assumes a position of submission vis-à-vis the Moroccan, that he subverts prevailing cultural and ethnic patterns of hierarchy and makes possible an assault on the dominant culture as inscribed on his body. Goytisolo, however, never really relinquishes power to his "hypervirile Arab" since as masochist, as Sartre puts it, he "ultimately treats the Other as an object and transcends him toward his own objectivity" (*Being and Nothingness* 493). Though Goytisolo discovers in the mirror that this objectivity, as an integrated and essential gay identity, is at best transitory, he remains unaware that his action reasserts, despite its surreptitious disturbance of gender, the preeminence of the bourgeois white European.

As autobiographer, Goytisolo nevertheless recognizes the contradictions intrinsic to the Don Julián project. Through the guise of Don Julián he seeks to silence his oppressors, but as he intimates with regard to his battle against the ever-present censor of Francoist Spain, his is a Pyrrhic victory (*RT* 25) in that the din raised by his discursive attacks muffles the sought-after voice of gay authenticity, reinforcing hetero-relationality and hampering the realization of homo-reciprocity. In prefiguring the homobiographical writing that will follow the completion of the autobiographies, he announces the possibility of a new "cartography" and "speleology" that will free him from his "precious strangeness" (i.e., the stance of the lone warrior) and articulate a "similarity of experiences" (*RT* 306). From the perspective of the present, moreover, he sees the identity of Don Julián as entirely alien:

> El que ve y el que es visto forman uno en ti mismo, dice Mawlana; pero el expatriado de quien ahora te despides es *otro* y cuando haga su maleta y desaparezca de la ciudad a la que discretamente llegó en el efímero dulzor otoñal podrá flaubertianamente exclamar en el fervor de su empresa, confundido del todo con el felón de la remota leyenda, don Julián *c'est moi.* (*RT* 309)

> [The one who sees and the one who is seen are one within yourself, says Mawlana; but the expatriate you now bid farewell to is *another,* and when he packs his case and disappears from the city to which he came quietly in the ephemeral sweetness of autumn he could exclaim, à la Flaubert, in the fever of his undertaking, totally at one with the felon in the distant legend: don Julián, *c'est moi.* (*RS* 261)]

As Jo Labanyi argues, by embedding the autobiographical self in a double intertextual reference to *Reivindicación del Conde don Julián* and *Madame*

Bovary, Goytisolo in fact denies the existence of the natural self on which traditional autobiography (and lesbian and gay life writing) is predicated (215). According to the final paragraph of *En los reinos de taifa,* autobiographers attempt to confer on the past a teleological structure that it lacks, yet they ultimately fail because of the insufficiency of language to grasp lived experience and traverse "la infranqueable distancia del hecho a lo escrito" (*RT* 309) ["the unbridgeable distance between act and written word" (*RS* 261)]. Goytisolo thus maintains a distinction between language and life, all the while aware that this distinction is itself an illusion: "el silencio y sólo el silencio mantendrá intacta una pura y estéril ilusión de verdad" (*RT* 309) ["silence, silence alone will keep intact a pure, sterile illusion of truth" (*RS* 261)]. Goytisolo, of course, avoids the even more subtle illusion of silence and continues to write. His emphasis, however, shifts from the revindication of an individual gay identity to the elucidation of a common gay praxis. As his autobiographies demonstrate, the Gordian knot of hetero-relationality can never be permanently cut. New and more positive bonds of homo-relationality, nonetheless, can and will be constructed.

CHAPTER THREE

Jaime Gil de Biedma

The Impossibility of Ithaca

When Jaime Gil de Biedma died of AIDS in 1990, he had long since ceased his poetic meditation on "el paso del tiempo y yo,"[1] leaving behind no testimony of his final struggle against time and the dissolution of the self through the cataclysmic epidemic of the late twentieth century. Yet his views on the relationship of disease to temporal subjectivity and the writing self were clarified several decades earlier through his experience with the great nineteenth-century plague, tuberculosis, recounted in the *Diario del artista seriamente enfermo* [Diary of the seriously ill artist] of 1974 and in the amplified 1991 version of it, *Retrato del artista en 1956* [Portrait of the artist in 1956].[2] Though all of Gil de Biedma's writing contains autobiographical elements, the *Retrato* is significant within his corpus insofar as it is the only text in which he employs the formal paradigms of autobiographical discourse. It is nonetheless a hybrid piece, primarily a diary but also a self-portrait and autobiography as well as a collection of personal letters, poems (his own and others'), photographs, and brief commentaries on art and politics. This shifting, fluid structure reveals Gil de Biedma's effort, and his eventual failure, to grasp a fixed and essential self. His serious illness is thus not tuberculosis (in his case an almost benevolent affliction easily cured through antibiotic treatment), but the crisis of self-representation present in the gay autobiographies of Roig and Goytisolo and in much postmodernist writing. Whereas tuberculosis might be seen with hindsight as a prelude to AIDS, the *Retrato* really prefigures the death of the poet persona depicted in the *Poemas póstumos* [Posthumous poems] and concomitantly of the "grand narrative" of the self on which modern autobiography as a genre is predicated.[3] Notwithstanding that, it can also be read as an early expression of his concern for the disaffected masses (both Spanish and Filipino) and the beginning of his period of social commitment.[4]

Like a traditional autobiographer, Gil de Biedma conflates the writing and written selves, but time, as he conceives of it, precludes what the phenomenologist critic John Claude Curtin calls the autobiographer's "diastolic gathering together of intentional multiplicity" (344). At the outset, Gil de Biedma posits time as an external force separating the self of the present from the self of the past, only to determine that time arises through the very act of writing, constituting the written self as past and hence always as other than the writing self. He strives to sustain an illusion of ontological identity with the written self, but identity is shattered at the moment of its genesis. As Roberta Quance writes with regard to Gil de Biedma's poet persona, "the self exists as it recedes" (292).

The *Retrato* is in fact characterized by an epistemological uncertainty crystallized in the pronouncement "no sé quién soy" (17) [I do not know who I am].[5] Gil de Biedma attempts to lay claim to the title of poet and affirm it as his intrinsic identity: "mi vida ha estado y está determinada desde los diecinueve años por la idea fija de que yo era, de que yo he de ser poeta" (62) [my life has been determined since the age of nineteen by the fixed idea that I was, that I must be a poet]. But in making this assertion he hesitates, wavering between essentialist and constructionist views of the self and revealing the contradiction inherent in any appeal to ontological sincerity: that to be true to himself he must become what he already is.[6] Gil de Biedma sees himself mandated from within but is filled with self-doubt and anxiety. He insists that he possesses the intelligence, experience, sensitivity, verbal gift, curiosity, and passion required of a poet (62), all the while experiencing dismay at the spectacle of what he calls his own unbearable and chronic incapacity (62). At times he questions the existence of a fixed identity underlying the image he projects for others and speaks of his persona as "una imitación falsa de tanta falsedad que el original acaba por resultarme también sospechoso" (55) [a false imitation of so much falsity that the original also ends up seeming suspect to me]. Yet he remains resolute in his endeavor, convinced that the day he ceases to consider himself a poet, he will for all intents and purposes cease to exist (62). In this context he arrives at the premature conclusion that the *Retrato* itself is no more than a distraction and an excuse for not writing poems, whereas in reality it will continue to function as a primary instrument of self-expression long after his abandonment of poetry.

The *Retrato* resists easy categorization within the various autobiographical genres. Gil de Biedma describes it in the following way:

> un instrumento de control de mí mismo, un modo de ponerme un poco en orden y también de moverme hacia actitudes que por imperativos de orden intelectual o moral creo que debo adoptar. *Most of [the time] I am trying to teach myself either to think or to behave — or both — in a way which I think is the right one for me.* (66–67)

> [an instrument of self-control, a way of putting myself somewhat in order and also of moving toward attitudes that for intellectual or moral imperatives I believe that I should adopt . . .]

In this passage Gil de Biedma assumes the stance of a diarist, and in keeping with the generic distinctions proposed by Georges May, initiates an act of self-exploration through reflection on his day-to-day activities. Though gay life writers such as Roig often employ a diary format as a means of articulating a gay identity, Gil de Biedma actually came to terms with his sexuality prior to the inception of his life writing enterprise. The *Retrato* is neither a coming-out narrative nor a defense of gay sexuality, and for these reasons it lacks the apologetic and confessional tendencies found in both Roig's and Goytisolo's works. Nonetheless, Gil de Biedma devotes considerable portions of his journal to meditations on his sexuality and relationships with men, as well as to certain social conditions of gay sexuality.

Gil de Biedma recalls keeping a diary as early as 1950, but it was not until a trip to the Philippines in 1956 that he launched the project culminating in the *Retrato*. The opening section of the text, "Las islas de Circe" [The islands of Circe], was written in the Philippines during the first half of the year. (Gil de Biedma, who worked in the Spanish office of the Compañía General de Tabacos de Filipinas [General Company of Philippine Tobaccos], had been sent to study Philippine labor, fiscal, and corporate law and to participate in the reorganization of the company's local offices.) It is followed by the official report of his visit. The third section, "De regreso en Itaca" [Back in Ithaca], covers the second half of the year after Gil de Biedma returned to Spain and was diagnosed with tuberculosis. Except for several minor changes, it is identical to the *Diario del artista seriamente enfermo* of 1974. Whereas "De regreso en Itaca" was first published eighteen years after its original composition, "Las islas de Circe" was withheld for a period of three and a half decades, until 1991. Not only is it the more recently published of the two texts, but its explicit treatment of gay sexuality also stands in sharp contrast to the aesthetic and philosophical ruminations of "De regreso en Itaca."

"Las islas de Circe" and "De regreso en Itaca" are thematically linked through the Homeric imagery of the titles. Gil de Biedma describes a circular trajectory, from Spain (Ithaca) to the Philippine archipelago (the islands of Circe) and home again. In this framework Ithaca represents the unity of family and state, and from the gay perspective of Gil de Biedma, the prevailing social structures of heterosexuality. The islands of Circe, on the other hand, indicate both Gil de Biedma's geographic displacement and his libidinal dispersion through a series of male lovers whose "enchantment" consists in diverting his attention from the construction of his identity as a poet. While a primary goal of the Homeric poem is reintegration within family and state, the aim of the *Retrato* is the realization of the self. Yet in the end the identity of Gil de Biedma remains fragmented: the islands of Circe are not constituted into a harmonious whole as suggested by the Hart Crane verse "adagios of islands."[7] This latter image, which appears at various critical junctures in the *Retrato,* in fact functions as a leitmotif, haunting Gil de Biedma's entire autobiographical undertaking as the promise of an impossible ontological fulfillment.

"De regreso en Itaca" follows "Las islas de Circe" according to the internal chronology of the *Retrato* as well as through its progressive concealment of homoerotic desire. Gil de Biedma writes openly of his sexuality in "Las islas de Circe," but throughout most of his writing career he avoids a direct revelation of his sexual life. The social conditions of Francoist Spain impeded the printing of expressly homoerotic material, and as he recognized in 1956, the Philippine diary was unpublishable at the time of its composition (134). But Gil de Biedma eschewed confessional writing in general, as Dionisio Cañas maintains, "porque el patetismo autoconfesional le parecía obsceno y de mal gusto" (28) [because self-confessional pathos seemed to him obscene and in bad taste (trans. mine)]. Nonetheless, though homoerotic desire is veiled in his poetry,[8] his ostensible attitude toward confessional writing is somewhat disingenuous, especially since "Las islas de Circe" is itself a kind of gay testimony. Yet it was not until the end of his life, in the face of changing social mores and the ravages of AIDS, that Gil de Biedma decided to make available to the reading public the homoerotic portion of his life writing, and then only after his death.

The Islands of Circe

Whereas "De regreso en Itaca" describes the isolation of the self through illness, "Las islas de Circe" focuses on the self in relation to the other in the context of gay sexuality. With regard to his own identification as a gay man, Gil de Biedma writes that at the age of twenty, following a frustrated relationship with a friend, Juan Antonio, "decidí en toda deliberación pasarme al bando homosexual" [I decided after much deliberation to go over to the homosexual camp] and that "jamás me vino a las mientes que pudiera un día enamorarme de un ser del sexo femenino" (71) [it never occurred to me that I might one day fall in love with someone of the feminine sex]. However, on one occasion during his visit to the Philippines Gil de Biedma experiences sex with a woman, and later he forms a close friendship with a colleague's wife. As a result he comes to reflect on heterosexual marriage. He questions his assumption that gay marginalization is propitious to the vocation of a poet and wonders if in a monogamous relationship with a woman he might redirect toward writing the energy expended on his numerous lovers. (Oddly enough, he makes no mention of the possibility of a monogamous relationship with a man.) He thus differs from Goytisolo (and to a certain extent even Roig), who relates his maturation as a writer to the expression of his sexuality. Gil de Biedma nevertheless insists that in his case marriage would be a hypocrisy, expressing revulsion at the spectacle of married men secretly pursuing male lovers (71). In the end he reaffirms a gay orientation, though he views it as primarily affective: "Antes que homosexual soy rabiosamente homo-sentimental" [rather than homosexual I am fiercely homosentimental (71)]. As indicated elsewhere (Swansey and Enríquez 205), he regards homosentimentality as an emotional, as opposed to an exclusively sexual, predilection for the masculine. This homosentimentality, though for him constitutive of an identity, is subordinate to what he chooses to regard as his primary identity as a poet.

Gil de Biedma is aware of the differing semiotics of male relationships in Spain and the Philippines. When he first sees two Filipino men holding hands, he imagines that he has discovered his "nativo país soñado" (39) [dreamed-of native land] of gay liberation. But he quickly realizes that he is reading the scene through the eyes of a Spanish homosexual (39) and that the action of these men is merely a gesture of friendship. Still, he is struck by the words of a gay North American who asserts that in the Philippines "*not everybody is gay but everybody is game*" (40). While this comment exoticizes Filipinos by attributing to them a sexual spontaneity absent in their European and North American counterparts, Gil de Biedma realizes that European and North American notions of sexual identity are not wholly applicable to Philippine sexuality. As Frederick L. Whitam and Robin M. Mathy observe, Filipinos do not traditionally equate sexual activity with sexual identity or hold the "Anglo-Saxon folk belief that sexual orientation is contagious, [and] precariously balanced" (149); and when, for example, "straight" males have sex with other men for pay, they are unlikely to disparage their sexual partners or fear that as a result of their actions they themselves might be identified as "gay." To a certain degree this is suggestive of Latin American paradigms of sexuality, but in the Philippine case sexual relations between males are less apt to be defined in terms of a masculine/feminine, active/passive dichotomy.[9] Although Gil de Biedma does not explicitly analyze Philippine patterns of male sexuality, his recognition of its cultural determinants leads him to question the essentialism in which he himself was indoctrinated.

Because of his situation, Gil de Biedma is acutely sensitive to issues of race and to the difficulties inherent in interracial gay relationships. He denounces the racism of the Spanish and North American communities of the Philippines (11) and challenges the supposed color-blindness of his compatriots as a hypocrisy. For the first time, moreover, he finds himself objectified as a white: "Me abruma la continua incomodidad de sentirme un ser genérico, un blanco. No soy o no represento más que eso, y me humilla" (11) [I am overwhelmed by the constant discomfort of feeling like a generic being, a white. I am not, nor do I represent anything more than that, and it humiliates me]. Like Goytisolo, he is ashamed to be identified with Europeans ("uno no quiere reconocerse en ellos" [25] [one does not want to recognize oneself in them]), and he attempts to detach himself from his Iberian placenta (25) and to meet Filipinos. Race, however, remains for him the overdetermining factor in all Filipino-European social relations on the islands, mediating his own intimate associations with men and blurring whatever distinctions he might hope to maintain between his public and private lives.

Gil de Biedma is specifically attracted to his first Filipino friend, radio actor Chris de la Vera, by his sarcastic attitude toward Europeans. At the party where they meet, an Englishman congratulates Vera for a performance, to which he responds: *"It's a consequence of my oriental breeding, my way of saying: I subject"* (14). Unlike the Muslim lovers of Goytisolo, Vera is thus able to voice opposition through the very discourse of his oppression. With him, Gil de Biedma hopes to transcend the dynamics of race, but his efforts are continually thwarted. When the two men visit a bar catering to Filipinos, the patrons are puzzled to see Gil de Biedma enter, while in a European setting the customers consider the presence of Vera an appalling intrusion that they feel obliged to bear with grace (30). When alone, race seems to dominate their conversations:

> tan pronto estamos lo bastante bebidos nos lanzamos a una disquisición apasionada acerca de la imposibilidad de toda amistad sólida entre nosotros, se lamenta él de haber nacido esclavo, me desespero yo de haber nacido tirano y de trabajar en una sociedad que es un símbolo de tiranía, doy viento al sentimiento de culpabilidad racial que he adquirido desde que estoy aquí, él declara que mi simpatía no es otra cosa que una actitud protectora, le devuelvo yo la impertinencia, cada cual decide no ver más al otro y cuando la situación es ya imposible nos confesamos que ha sido una noche maravillosa y que somos hermanos — lo cual, por mi parte, es absolutamente cierto: le quiero mucho — ; una vez llegados a la *catharsis,* nos despedimos hasta la próxima vez. (30)

[as soon as we are sufficiently drunk we launch into a passionate argument on the impossibility of any solid friendship between ourselves, he laments having been born a slave, I despair having been born a tyrant and working in a society that is a symbol of tyranny, I air the feeling of racial guilt that I have acquired since being here, he declares that my sympathy is nothing more than a patronizing attitude, I return to him the impertinence, each one decides not to see the other again and when the situation has become impossible we confess that it has been a marvelous evening and that we are brothers — which for my part is absolutely true: I love him very much; once we have reached the catharsis, we bid farewell until the next time.]

Despite the ironic tone, Gil de Biedma and Vera recognize their racial legacies, and in light of their respective histories raise doubt about the possibility of ever achieving reciprocity. As if to atone for the past, Gil de Biedma tries to shoulder the guilt of the white race, a gesture of submission that for Vera disguises an even more subtle and pernicious form of racial domination. In the end Gil de Biedma is compelled to admit an uncertainty regarding the attitude of Vera, and only from his perspective do they part as brothers. (He later learns that Vera suspected him of being a spy for the tobacco company.) Gil de Biedma claims that a catharsis has been experienced, but the structures of race remain intact at the end. In fact it is explicitly through race, rather than the masculine/feminine posturing of Goytisolo and his Muslim lovers, that the relationship of Vera and Gil de Biedma is hetero-ized and alienated.

Of all of Gil de Biedma's Filipino friends and lovers, Vera is the most attuned to political and social issues. The others — Pepe, Salvador, Lino, Pat, and Jay — appear in the *Retrato* as one-dimensional figures. Gil de Biedma reveals them against the backdrop of his personal life, but they rarely express a voice of their own or reflect on their lives except as they relate to his, and then almost exclusively in the context of sex. There are nevertheless exceptions. On one occasion, for example, Gil de Biedma describes an encounter with a young Chinese man named John, whom he meets during a brief trip to Hong Kong. Though John is ostensibly straight, he invites Gil de Biedma to spend the night with him. When they reach the room that John shares with his brother — a tiny cubicle too small to stand in — Gil de Biedma is overcome by his poverty and confused about his intentions: "Por un momento me pareció que John me miraba con cierta ironía reticente, pensé si le complacía mostrarme su absoluta indigencia, hacerme los honores de su miseria" (60) [For a moment it seemed that John was looking at me with a certain reticent irony, I wondered if it pleased him to show me his absolute indigence, to do me the honors of his misery]. This ironizing look differs from the assaultive look of Goytisolo's masculine Moroccan in that it subtly subverts European dominance rather than replicating the violence through which that dominance is sustained. Gil de Biedma considers leaving, but decides to stay so that he can maintain intact his sense of personal decency. During a sleepless night on the floor, he desperately desires to escape, finally concluding that escape is a luxury impossible for John and countless others like him.

While episodes such as this might be seen to betray the self-indulgent guilt of the wealthy European perhaps already detected by Vera, Gil de Biedma focuses not only on the self, as is so often the case with diary writers, but also on the social conditions of others, repeatedly attacking the European and North American treatment of Filipino farm workers, whose situation in the fields, he contends, differs little from slavery (73–74). More significant are the comments he makes in official contexts. In the report on the tobacco company, for instance, he denounces the discriminatory hiring procedures of the local administration and argues that the company can remain viable in the future only if it integrates Filipinos into managerial positions. He regards its exclusionary practice as a remnant of the colonial past and inefficient to the extent that it fails to utilize employees to their fullest capacity. (As an example he cites the case of a Filipina certified public accountant assigned to work part-time as a secretary and part-time as a purchase order clerk.) Elsewhere in the *Retrato* he discloses his own position as a Marxist fellow traveler, and though he questions Marxist politics of the period, he insists on the need to remedy the abuses of the neo-imperialist capitalism of the Philippines.

The Voyage of Return

Gil de Biedma ends "Las islas de Circe" with a description of his preparations to leave the Philippines and begins "De regreso en Itaca" with a narration of his journey home to Spain. He is in the aircraft, having lost sight of land and struggling to reconstruct the geographical and personal figures he has left behind — "la costa prolongándose" [the coast as it stretched away] and "Jay, lágrimas en los ojos" (117) [Jay, tears in his eyes].[10] (Jay is the only

Filipino lover mentioned in this section of the *Retrato,* and likely the one with whom Gil de Biedma was most closely bonded.) But as the shift in tense reveals, he almost immediately assumes the perspective of the past: "Hoy, después del almuerzo, al cogerme Jay la mano, la intimidad física me ha parecido algo tan extraño y tan involuntario como la separación. No queda tiempo para hacer el amor, no queda nada para decirnos" (117) [To-day, after lunch, when Jay took my hand, the physical intimacy seemed as strange and as involuntary as our separation. There is no time left to make love, there is nothing left to say to each other]. Yet in the past in question, time is already escaping ("no queda tiempo") and with it goes the possibility of narrativizing the self in reciprocity with the other ("no queda nada para decirnos"). Gil de Biedma remains detached in his ruminations, hovering as it were in midair, but manages to locate a connecting thread to the self when he recalls perceiving a familiar scent during a final walk through Manila: "De paso por San Luis, camino del Casino, reconozco de pronto un olor y casi me detengo. El olor de los barrios humildes del litoral de España: pes-cado frito" (118) [Passing along San Luis, on my way to the casino, I suddenly recognize a smell and I almost stop. The smell of the humble neighborhoods of the Spanish coast: fried fish]. He then describes a series of scents that leads him, in Proustian fashion, closer to home and to a vision of the past: "Olor a escarcha y fuego de leña verde, pavesas en el aire. La Nava, años de la guerra civil, camino de la escuela en las mañanas" (118) [The smell of frost and a green-wood fire, sparks in the air. La Nava, the years of the Civil War, on my way to school in the morning]. Gil de Biedma is abruptly drawn back to the present when a flight attendant offers him a drink. But the key to the self has been identified: the homeland, to which he now returns, and the Casa de Caño, the family estate in Nava de la Asunción, in the province of Segovia, where he will spend his convalescence.

While recuperating from his illness, Gil de Biedma experiences a new sense of time and as a consequence commences a lengthy meditation on the temporal structure of the self. He views time in the city as linear and causal:

En Barcelona el pasado es irreversible y sucesivo, se ordena por jornadas: cuando recuerdo alguna, la veo como una etapa previa a la siguiente, necesa-rias ambas para haber llegado a hoy. El presente anula el pasado porque es su consecuencia, porque lo agota. (146)

[In Barcelona the past is irreversible and successive, it is ordered in days: when I remember one, I see it as a step previous to the following one, both necessary to have arrived at today. The present annuls the past because it is its consequence, because it exhausts it.]

In this temporal scheme, events are inherently necessary, although their teleological structure reveals itself only retrospectively from the vantage point of the present. In contrast, time in the country is hypostatized in discrete moments: "Aquí el tiempo se deposita en estratos intactos, diferenciados y suficientes: cada uno es como una isla griega. Ninguna imagen más lejana, ninguna más borrosa, todas durando en el mismo ámbito. *Adagios of islands*" (146) [Here time is deposited in intact strata, differentiated and self-sufficient: each one is like a Greek island. No one image more distant, no one more indistinct, all enduring in the same expanse. Adagios of islands]. The process of temporal hypostatization is expressed intertextually through the Crane metaphor, in which distinct geographical entities (first discerned by Gil de Biedma from the airplane window during a flight over the Philippines, but now read as blocks of past time and hence as fragments of the self) are slowly dematerialized into a musical cadence. They are then reconstituted as a montage of simultaneous past images:

Aquella noche me veía a mí mismo, a la vez, en cien momentos distintos, repetido, variado e idéntico. Lo mismo que esas pinturas del *cuattrocento* que presentan simultáneamente con todo detalle, con toda independencia, pero ordenados dentro de un único espacio, los episodios sucesivos de una historia. (146)

[That night I saw myself, at the same time, in a hundred different moments, repeated, varied, and identical. The same as those paintings from the *cuattrocento* that present simultaneously, with full detail, with full independence, but ordered within a single space, the successive episodes of a story.][11]

Gil de Biedma thus imagines the country to be a site of timelessness through which the self, heretofore alienated by the "disease" of temporal displacement, is united and made whole.

It is specifically through scents and odors that the recovery of the self begins: "El retorno empezó en Madrid, con el olor del aire" (146) [The return (both to La Nava and to the past) began in Madrid, with the scent of the air]. At La Nava, Gil de Biedma comes to see, and actually smell, the world as he did as a child, and in describing his room he speaks of "un butacón tapizado de cuero, y su olor a persona mayor" (147) [an armchair upholstered in leather, with its grown-up scent]. His identification with the past, however, remains incomplete — "la intensidad ya no es la misma" (148) [the intensity is no longer the same] — and he gradually becomes aware of the impossibility of ever achieving a veritable return. He indicates that he spent his last summer of ontological plenitude — "mi última larga temporada de Hijo de Dios" (148) [my last long season as Son of God] — in La Nava in 1950, at the age of twenty. Since then, his life has changed irrevocably, and his subsequent visits have been no more than "attempted returns" (148).[12] To a certain degree this is the result of a deepening self-reflexivity that autobiographical writing ultimately serves only to exacerbate.

Gil de Biedma admits having been obsessed with the notion of "momentos vividos que creía imborrables" (149) [lived moments I thought to be indelible] and in recent years with nurturing a dream of returning to the past, to an evening in the month of May 1948. He believed this was possible insofar as he mistakenly endowed time with a dimension of spatiality. If he could orient himself in space through a physical object, why could he not do the same in time through a particular moment, approaching or withdrawing from it at will? All that was necessary (as in the case of the "perfect moments" described by Sartre in the novel *Nausea*) was a certain attitude: "Era sólo cuestión de estar alerta, sabiendo qué buscaba, y de propiciar la suerte — o sea: de observar ritos" (149) [It was only a question of being alert, knowing what I was looking for, and of creating a propitious condition or, rather, of observing rites]. Now he considers such an endeavor futile, no longer envisioning the moments of the past as fixed but as perpetually moving and changing, continually melted down and recast through the unrelenting mediation of the present. The perfect moment experienced by the youth in the spring of 1948 is in fact unknowable to the extent that it discloses itself only through the avatar of the adult of 1956: "De qué sirve que regrese la exaltación que conocí aquella noche de 1948, al pie de la escalinata de la Iglesia de Sitges, junto al mar, si ya no sé que es ella" (149) [What does it matter if the exaltation I felt that night of 1948, at the foot of the steps of the church of Sitges, at the edge of the sea, were to return, if I no longer even recognize it].

After acknowledging the destruction of this fundamental moment through the "horrible dynamism" (149) of real time, Gil de Biedma launches an even more thorough introspection of his past. In the process he abandons the stance of diarist and assumes the position of autobiographer, adopting a perspective on his entire life rather than simply on the immediate period in which he is writing. As autobiographer, he reveals that his earliest memory is of his own voice: "Mi más temprano recuerdo nítido es el de oír mi voz en la penumbra de la siesta, en Barcelona, en el cuarto que da a la galería, preguntando a Modesta cuándo iríamos a San Rafael" (149–50) [My earliest clear memory is of hearing my voice in the semi-darkness of the siesta, in Barcelona, in the room that opens onto the gallery, asking Modesta (family servant and nanny) when we would go to San Rafael]. At first glance, the enunciation of his voice seems to precede that of the other. Yet despite the apparent primacy of the subject, the act involves a temporal and reflective distancing with regard to an even earlier moment. Indeed, the child already knows the answer: "lo que importa es que recuerdo haber sabido de antemano que iríamos a San Rafael, en junio, y que mi pregunta obedecía sólo al deseo de incorporar mi certeza en alguna forma de realidad sensible" (150) [what matters is that I remember having known beforehand that we would go to San Rafael in June and that my question corresponded solely to the desire to incorporate my certainty into some form of sensible reality]. What Gil de Biedma remembers is itself a recollection of something articulated elsewhere and before — the plans of the bourgeois family for a summer holiday in the mountains. His self-reflexivity thus arises through an internalization of the discourse of the other. The upshot, which he slowly comes to realize, is that the self that he hoped to recover was never entirely his to lose.

Gil de Biedma abruptly terminates his autobiographical interlude and returns to the present time, commenting on the Suez crisis and the response of the international community. This jarring shift betrays a disillusion with the past and with the attempt to recapture an inherent, essential self. Not only is his past beyond reach — "ni siquiera me identifico del todo con los recuerdos, a pesar de cómo me poseen aquí" (154) [I don't even identify completely with my memories, in spite of how they possess me here] — but so too is his very sense of identity — "Creo que he perdido el sentimiento de mí mismo" (154) [I believe that I have lost the sense of myself]. This loss of self is at least in part the result of his isolation through illness. Just as his ideas are formulated only in conjunction with those of others — "dejado a mí mismo, no pensaría — y probablemente tampoco escribiría — casi nunca" (185) [left to myself, I would almost never think, and probably I would not write either] — his entire identity hinges on a larger societal discourse. For this reason his solitary self-reflection leads nowhere and ultimately reflects nothing: "Llevo un rato largo de mirar por la ventana, intentando imaginarme a mí mismo ahora mismo, sin ningún éxito" (153) [I have been looking out the window for a long while, trying to imagine myself right now, without any success]. The "health" achieved in the country is therefore not a transcendence of temporal fragmentation but is instead an illusion of wholeness concealing a fundamental and inescapable alienation.

Gil de Biedma is progressively disabused of his former notion of an autonomous and fixed self, and as he emerges from the cloistered world of his family estate, he turns his attention outward, feeling greater solidarity with the Spanish people and particularly those of the working classes who suffered the most as a consequence of the Civil War. The subsequent passages of "De regreso en Itaca" thus focus less on his personal past and more on that of others, and his observations of the Spanish class structure in fact parallel his comments on race in "Las islas de Circe" and his report on the tobacco company. He begins writing the silent history of the town of La Nava, known before 1936 as a center of socialist activity. He further gives voice to Modesta and her recollections of prewar Madrid, of intellectual and popular luminaries such as Unamuno and Gloria Laguna, and of his own family members. He includes Modesta's anecdotes, songs, and reflections on life and politics. In contrast, he observes his family through a highly critical lens. Following the portrait of Modesta, for example, he reveals his parents' intransigent refusal to support the return of war refugees from the Soviet Union. As a child of the victors, moreover, he claims that he and others like him have been limited in their scope of thought and action. For Gil de Biedma, however, poetry becomes a way of traversing barriers and connecting with others, and through an analysis of the relationship between the reader and the writer of the poetic text, he comes to discern the possibilities of a poetry of social commitment.

This heightened sense of reciprocity is coupled with a waning of the autobiographical persona. Impersonal entries hold the promise of subjective integration: "Tranquilidad. Encontrar en la cama otro cuerpo, después de tantos meses de dormir solo, temía que nuevamente me disparase. Todo va bien, por ahora" (205) [Peace. Finding another body in bed, after so many months of sleeping alone, I feared I might run off again. Everything is going all right, so far].[13] But in the final pages of "De regreso en Itaca," which coincide with the end of the 1956 calendar year, Gil de Biedma describes "una conciencia difusa de final anonimato" (206) [a diffuse consciousness of final anonymity]. Once again in Barcelona, he looks from his office window at the Christmas lights and the throngs of pedestrians on the Ramblas and feels as if he were a survivor. What he has survived is precisely himself, and what remains is a cipher among many, flickering for a moment like the artificial lights in the city night.

"De regreso en Itaca" closes on an ambiguous note: it is the beginning of a new year, but odd numbered years, Gil de Biedma fears, might well be the most sterile ones. He will continue to write, no longer in the hope of recovering the amorphous self of the past, but of inscribing through poetry the identity of the poet. As he later reveals, he will eventually aspire to become not a poet but a poem: "yo creía que quería ser poeta, pero en el fondo quería ser poema" (qtd. in Persin 285) [I believed that I wanted to be a poet, but deep down I wanted to be a poem (trans. mine)]. Yet in Gil de Biedma the projects of the poet and the autobiographer are synonymous to the extent that both use language as a means of constituting a unified self. Both, however, fail, with the self forever fragmented in a state of discursive diaspora. Gil de Biedma's goal of return from egological exile remains no more than an intertext — "el protagonista, al final, volvía a casa" (150) [the protagonist, in the end, returned home], and as such is an echo of countless classical and modernist texts (including his first childhood reading of the adventures of Captain Gilson in *La pagoda de cristal* [The crystal pagoda]) through which he attempts to situate himself but which in fact function to situate him in a state of perpetual alterity. He aims in the *Retrato* to draw his portrait of the artist as a young man, but ultimately his subject eludes him. As in Roig's and Goytisolo's works, his "inscription" of the self, though less focused on its sexual specificity, leads (homographically) to a "description" of the self. The gay autobiographies of Roig, Goytisolo, and Gil de Biedma thus undermine the essentialistic preconceptions of traditional lesbian and gay life writing. For this reason, moreover, they all prefigure, in spite of the explicit intentions of the three autobiographers themselves, the postmodern aesthetic of the queer.

PART 2

Queer Autobiography

Luis Antonio de Villena

Camping-It-Up in the Francoist Camp

Whereas gay autobiographers attempt through language both to reveal and realize an identity that is itself irreducible to language, queer life writers play at identity through a language that ultimately functions as a kind of drag. They too are often haunted by the desire for a fixed and natural gay self, but the emphasis in their writing is on the performance rather than the essence of identity. This move from essence to performance "lightens" their writing to the extent that it is carried out through shifting and incongruous (and as such humorous) representations of gender and sexuality. What is more, queer life writers not only play at identity but are less apt than their gay counterparts to take seriously the conventional requirements of the autobiographical genre. If the self is conceived of as a fiction, then so too is its history. In contrast to the autobiographical personae of Roig, Goytisolo, and Gil de Biedma, those of Villena, Moix, and Almodóvar are, to a certain degree at least, explicitly "made up." Yet like the former three life writers, the latter express an uneasiness in the face of their egological instability and dispersion through the text. This is because all, despite their differing responses to their condition, are obliged to navigate the same discursive terrain of hetero-relationality.

Villena is both a poet and a prose writer, and like Gil de Biedma his entire corpus contains elements of self-representation.[1] He prefaces his memoir of adolescence, *Ante el espejo* [Before the mirror],[2] with the words of Rousseau: "Je sais bien que le lecteur n'a pas grand besoin de savoir tout cela, mais j'ai besoin, moi, de le lui dire" (5) [I am well aware that the reader has no great need to know all this, but I have a need to tell it to him]. In so doing he situates his "life" within the context of classic Western autobiography while at the same time disclosing a desire, echoed by numerous lesbian and gay life writers, to give social visibility to his sexuality. Aspects of *Ante el espejo* are nevertheless patently fictitious. The name of the narrator, for example, is not Luis but Felipe, and the year of his birth is 1949, not 1951. Villena thus breaks the autobiographical pact according to which author, narrator, and protagonist are presumed to be identical and gradually dissociates himself from his autobiographical persona. He does this as part of "un intento de cortar, de independizarme por completo del niño y del muchacho que fui y gritarle en la distancia: '*¡Ya no me perteneces!*' " (131–32) [an effort to cut and to liberate myself completely from the child and youth that I was and to shout at him in the distance: "*You no longer belong to me!*"]. At the outset Villena in fact holds an essentialist conception of the self, but in the end he subverts the ideology of identity through a continuous and subtle parodying. He therefore uses his memoir as a mirror that not only reflects but also rescripts and reconfigures the past. Like the queer child posing before his mother's looking glass, the adult life writer "camps-it-up" in *Ante el espejo,* denaturalizing the social milieu through which he, as a gay man and aristocrat, was initially constituted as unnatural. Though he fails to achieve the naturalness for which he longed throughout his youth — "la adolescencia le quedaría siempre como una privación, como el robo que un desconocido ladrón le había cometido" (130) [adolescence would remain forever like a privation, like a robbery committed by an unknown thief],[3] he eventually comes to represent himself not as the victim of an ontological theft but as the agent of his own difference.

Queer Performativity and the Aesthetics of Camp

Villena's self-representation as a nonheterosexual and nonbourgeois within the framework of Francoist Spain reveals a camp aesthetic that current queer theory can help to inform. Moe Meyer, in the groundbreaking collection of essays *The Poetics and Politics of Camp,* defines camp as "the total body of performative practices and strategies used to enact a queer identity, with enactment defined as the production of social visibility" (5).[4] Despite his use of the term "identity," he regards camp not as an essence residing within human beings or things but as an act as well as a way of reading and of writing "that originates in the 'Camp eye'" (13). In short, it is a form of parody. In keeping with Anthony Giddens's argument that power and dominance rest on the ability to produce codes of signification (31), Meyer conceptualizes parody as an instrument through which the marginalized and disenfranchised enter alternate codes into the dominant discourse. Whereas the "original" marks the site of dominance, parody, and "Camp, as specifically queer parody, becomes . . . the only process by which the queer is able to enter representation and to produce social visibility" (11). Because of this "piggybacking" on dominant structures of signification, camp appears to reinforce and to undermine the prevailing heterosexual ideology simultaneously (Meyer 11). Camp nonetheless refuses to derive a fixed identity from its performances, and according to Meyer, "it is precisely in the space of this refusal, in the deconstruction of the homo/hetero binary," that the threat and challenge of queer sexuality "is queerly executed" (3).

The autobiography of Villena functions as a "camp eye" that destabilizes dominant bourgeois configurations of gender and social class and turns homosexual and aristocratic posturing into acts of defiance. According to Thomas A. King, bourgeois ideology, as articulated in the seventeenth and eighteenth centuries, in fact conflated the two terms. An aristocratic demeanor was viewed as an appearance that lacked the ontological foundation necessary for moral rectitude and material progress and ultimately was seen as effeminate, insofar as bourgeois notions of selfhood were negotiated on an implicitly male body (26). As a consequence, the "residual elements of [the] performative [aristocratic] self were transcoded as markers of homosexuality" (23). Unlike the effete aristocrat, however, the homosexual (specifically for King the seventeenth- and eighteenth-century English molly), through his "sin that could not be named," chose to occupy a nonspace outside of the divinely created order of nature. In so doing, King argues, he did not take on a new identity but instead executed an "(un)identification with the normative models of self mandated by the increasingly dominant bourgeoisie" (41). To counter this threat to established social identifications, the bourgeoisie attempted to ossify queer praxis by ascribing to it a fixed identity of deviance.

Villena himself detects a queer praxis in the figure of the nineteenth-century dandy, and in the collection of essays titled *Corsarios de guante amarillo: Sobre el dandysmo* [Corsairs of the yellow glove: On dandyism], he examines the interconnectedness of gender and class performativity. He holds that the dandy, like the aristocrat, trivializes bourgeois notions of productivity and utilitarianism. Yet he sees him as a rebel, flaunting conventional codes of behavior and repudiating the values of all social classes. Though frequently identified with gay sexuality, the dandy is not intrinsically gay, and his homoerotic activity is but one of various acts of rebellion (24). To the extent that he is classifiable in sexual categories at all, he is a narcissist and exhibitionist who uses the other as a means of asserting his own difference (23). Villena thus identifies a sadistic streak at the heart of his apparent passivity and masochism. There is also, it might be added, a fundamental contradiction: the dandy refuses bourgeois essentialization while at the same time affirming a radical bourgeois individualism that precludes homosolidarity or the construction of homo-relationality. As Villena points out, the dandy is antidemocratic and oblivious to the collectivist principles of socialism. He nevertheless believes that the dandy's individualism represents a significant challenge to the choke of contemporary mass culture.[5]

In *Corsarios* Villena reveals having been obsessed with the figure of the dandy: "en unos años, constituyó para mí como un *trabajo,* como un obligado camino en la autoexpresión" (163) [for some years it constituted for me a *task,* an obligatory path in self-expression]. In *Ante el espejo* he takes stock of his past as "un niño triste y de corbatas lila" (*Corsarios* 163) [a sad boy with lilac ties], recognizing and validating his camp posturing while nonetheless agonizing over his supposed unnaturalness.[6] Whereas the dandy aspires to achieve an aesthetic "beyond nature" (*Corsarios* 11), Villena has been constituted as unnatural through the action of an unnamed societal other, the "desconocido ladrón" [unknown thief], who is specifically the bourgeois male heterosexual. Villena desires to reject and to emulate this figure simultaneously, and as a consequence *Ante el espejo* is charged with a tension between an affirmation of unnaturalness and a yearning for an ever-elusive naturalness discerned in childhood scenes of masculine camaraderie. In the end, however, he renounces his search for the natural and adopts a position similar to that of the quintessential exponent of *fin-de-siècle* dandyism, Oscar Wilde, whose inversion of the natural/unnatural binary opposition, according to the deconstructionist analysis of Jonathan Dollimore, calls into question the entire doctrine of identity on which bourgeois morality and compulsory heterosexuality are founded. In contrast to such critics as Robert Young, for whom an inversion of terms merely perpetuates the binary that it aims to displace (87), Dollimore argues that inversion is necessary if an eventual displacement of the binary is ever to be achieved: "simply to jump beyond it into a world free of it, is simply to leave the binary intact in the only world we have" (66). For Rita Felski, on the other hand, the transgressive aesthetic of Wilde that for Dollimore subverts the "organicist ideals of the authentic and natural self" (Felski 1099) applies solely to the male subject. In a figure such as Wilde, therefore, "femininity signifies an unsettling of automatized perceptions of gender, whereas feminine qualities in a woman merely confirm her incapacity to escape her natural condition" (1099). This contradiction is in fact present throughout Villena's comments on the masculine and the feminine.

Reflections of Masculinity and Femininity

Ante el espejo opens on a note of ambiguity. It begins with the statement, "Todo empezaba en una gran escalera oscura" (7) [It all began on a big, dark staircase]. Yet in the following sentence Villena suggests that the first image perceived by his infantile (camp) eye was the gleam of baubles: "Y aunque es más que posible que tenga recuerdos anteriores (el fulgor de las sortijas de la abuela o de mamá, acercándose a la cuna)" (7) [Although it is more than possible that I have earlier memories (the shine of Grandmother's or Mamma's rings as they approached the cradle)]. This primordial memory of sparkling gems, for the camp performer the epitome of feminine appearance, has been overshadowed by the memory of a darkened staircase, an image of both emptiness (the youthful experience of which Villena was deprived) and, through its verticality, the world of masculine hierarchy. In the course of his autobiographical venture he will unbracket and uncloset his femininity. In keeping with the nearest Spanish equivalent for the verb "to camp," he will "sacar la pluma" [get out the feather] — the "pluma" in his case being the "pen" of the adult life writer as well as the "feather" of his childhood drag, and as such his multifaceted appearances in the mirror. Ultimately, however, appearance will not be essentialized but will remain a performance, neither inherently masculine nor feminine, but dynamic and forever changing.

After an initial description of his grandmother's baronial mansion, an anachronism in bourgeois postwar Madrid, Villena presents three primary male figures from his childhood: a schoolmate named Fernando, his uncle Máximo, and his father. Fernando, an ice-hockey player and boy scout, represented the masculine youth that Villena hoped to know and imitate. But because of a "miedo a que se *diera cuenta*" (17) [fear that it (i.e., his homoerotic desire) might be *found out*], he felt unable to pursue the friendship that Fernando seemed willing to offer. He interprets his timidity as a self-destructive act resulting from an internalized homophobia: "Quemaba una parte de mí mismo — la mejor parte de mí mismo — en una de tantas hogueras como la Edad Media había visto y seguía viendo" (17) [I burned a part of myself — the best part of myself — in one of so many fires that the Middle Ages had seen and continued seeing]. This frustrated desire to establish reciprocity with the male other forms the backdrop of *Ante el espejo*.

Through the portrayals of his gay uncle and straight father, Villena reflects on male sexuality in both the prewar and Francoist generations. His father, an exaggeratedly virile figure, had rejected the monarchism of his aristocratic family and joined the Falangists. His uncle, in contrast, remained tied to the family and assumed the characteristics of a dandy. He never worked, and in summarizing his activities Villena cites Lord Henry's comment to Dorian Grey: "*tus días son tus sonetos*" (21) [*your days are your sonnets*]. What is more, his life ended in tragedy: at the outset of the Spanish Civil War he was mysteriously killed while en route to a rendezvous with a lover. Whereas this gay forebear perished, the straight father survived and thrived under fascism. As a child, nevertheless, Villena expressly revived the memory of his uncle and came to view him as "un decadente y nostálgico *ángel de la guarda*" (28) [a decadent and nostalgic *guardian angel*], who protected him in what for him was an alien heterosexual world. This in fact marked the beginning of his rescription of the past as well as his own gradual process of self-identification as a dandy.

Villena broaches the subject of his sexual identity through recollections of various female figures. As a child he saw his French governess, Isabelle, as the quintessence of femininity and loved and admired her so much that he began to imitate her: "me resultaba absolutamente atractiva, a tal punto, que cuando yo estaba solo, en mi cuarto o en cualquier otra habitación de la casa, fingía ser ella" (40) [she proved to be absolutely attractive to me, to such a degree that when I was alone, in my room or in any other room of the house, I pretended to be her]. He was similarly obsessed with female film celebrities, and in games with Clara, his cousin, he would assume the roles of his favorite heroines. These were his earliest and perhaps most fundamental expressions of camp. As David Bergman notes, "If the word *camp* is drawn from the French *camper,* to pose, to strike an attitude, then the drag performance is the essential act of the camp" (6). Despite his fascination with drag, however, Villena supposedly viewed his own identity as inherently masculine:

> yo no experimentaba deseos de *ser mujer* o de haber nacido mujer. No quería cambiar. Mi yo profundo fue siempre masculino, y puedo asegurar que me siento muy confortable en él. Pero mi yo externo, ese sí, se pensaba *estrella* y transformaba todo: mis pantalones en falda, mi reloj en brillantes, mi pañuelo en polvera. (44)

> [I experienced no desire *to be a woman* or to have been born a woman. I didn't want to change. My profound self was always masculine, and I can assure that I feel very comfortable in it. But my external self, that one, yes, thought of itself as a *star* and transformed everything: my pants into a skirt, my watch into diamonds, my handkerchief into a powder box.]

At this point in his narrative Villena struggles to affirm the existence of a masculine identity consubstantial with the facticity of maleness, yet in so doing he fails to account for the motivation behind the camp performances of his youth. His imitation of Isabelle might well have been an expression of affection, but his impersonation of popular icons of femininity was much more than a display of childhood infatuation. What he actually aimed to achieve was a degree of self-representation not possible for him within the rigorously masculine environment of his larger social sphere. As a consequence of his actions, moreover, he unwittingly undermined the masculine identity that he sought to claim as his own. This is because the parodic repetition of the "original" gender roles, in keeping with the analysis of Butler, "reveals the original to be nothing other than a parody of the *idea* of the natural and the original" (*Gender* 31; qtd. in Bergman 11).

It was at school that Villena became acutely aware of his difference. From the first day, certain boys regarded him with hostility and taunted him with the epithet "mariquita" [fairy]. On one occasion the students were assigned to write a description of a classmate they either liked or disliked. Afterward, the teacher had Villena collect the compositions. As he did so, he discovered that almost everyone had written about him, interpreting his body and movements and ascribing to him a series of feminine attributes that functioned to marginalize him. This episode is suggestive of the process whereby the gay male body, according to Edelman, is textualized as the nonmale: "Faced with gay men as the uncannily familiar and (therefore) intolerable mirror image of its own male-gendered face, heterosexual masculinity under patriarchy demands that the gay male body be interpreted, instead, as the other face of gender" (206). As a child, Villena was astounded by the judgments of his peers, but he never for a moment considered conforming to their standards:

> Me quedé sorprendido. Era yo una extrañeza para todos — favorable o nega-
> tivamente — y supe, sin razonármelo, que ése era *yo,* y que era así como debía
> seguir siendo. Es decir que ante el fervor o la hostilidad de la clase, nunca
> pensé en ser diferente, pensé que — en general — aquellos niños no tenían,
> para mí, interés ninguno. (58)

> [I was surprised. I was an oddity for everyone — whether favorably or nega-
> tively — and I knew, without reasoning it out, that that was *me,* and that I
> should go on being that way. That is to say, before the fervor or the hostility
> of the class, I never thought of being different, I thought that in general those
> boys were, for me, of no interest whatsoever.]

In this passage he views his identity as neither masculine nor feminine but simply as different: an oddity for everyone. Although he found his classmates uninteresting, he was less indifferent to them than he might have admitted at the time, and as he completed high school, he felt proud of his various accomplishments. To maintain his integrity in the face of explicit heterosexism required substantial resolve, and his fortitude left him with a lasting sense of satisfaction: "Me gusta ahora saber que el niño raro y dulce que fue tan atacado cuando llegó al colegio, supo defender su singularidad, y salió no menos raro, pero entre laureles" (65) [It pleases me to know now that the strange and sweet boy who was so attacked when he arrived at school, knew how to defend his singularity, and turned out no less strange, but in laurels].

In cultivating his role as "exotic flower" (56), Villena turned to writers of previous generations (Wilde, Proust, and the decadent poets on account of their elegance and outsiderness) and in particular to authors from the classical period. In his own earliest writings he imitated archaic genres, such as the pastoral novel, and came to envision a future as either a scholar of dead languages or, as would be the case with the young Moix, an Egyptologist. This fascination with the past and the exotic was symptomatic of his endeavor to fashion an identity unavailable to him in his immediate cultural milieu. Yet identity remained a performance, and whereas in his childhood games of make-believe he impersonated Isabelle and famous actresses, in high school he took up acting. A penchant for performing appears throughout his youth and continues in the present: "Actor he sido siempre. Cuando de niño jugaba con pendientes de mamá y trajes antiguos, y ahora también, puesto que muchas veces me represento" (63) [I have always been an actor. When as a child I played with Mamma's earrings and old gowns, and now as well, since I am often acting]. For Jack Babuscio, this theatricalization of experience derives in part from the exigency placed on gays to pass as straight (26). In the case of Villena, however, theatricality results not so much from an attempt to pass (despite his longing for naturalness), as from a concerted effort to cultivate his difference.

Villena's introduction to heterosexual masculinity occurred not only at school but also at a Falangist youth camp that his father forced him to attend at the age of ten. Thrust from the aristocratic and feminine milieu of his childhood home, Villena confronted the dynamics of popular Spanish machismo as incarnated in his fourteen-year-old section leader, the *Jefe,* and in the camp director. Through these figures, Villena rescripts the role of the patriarch (his father and ultimately the fascist dictator himself) and in so doing attempts to suspend and neutralize his power. He depicts the ostensibly heterosexual *Jefe* as an exhibitionist: "No tenía reparo alguno (es más, le gustaba) en hacer exhibiciones sexuales delante de nosotros. . . . Se rascaba y tocaba frecuentemente el sexo, a mi parecer ya grande, y lo exhibía erecto" (71)

[He had no misgivings whatsoever (in fact he enjoyed) making sexual exhibitions in front of us. . . . He would frequently scratch and touch his penis, in my opinion already large, and he displayed it erect]. This posturing on the part of the *Jefe,* coupled with the explicit observation of his body by both the camper child and the adult autobiographer, has the potential to denaturalize heterosexual masculinity. As Edelman writes: "The body, once subjected to the necessity of interpretation, becomes suddenly unnatural, its every feature questionable, its very mode theatrical; and in a culture committed to the ideological construction of maleness as the antithesis of representation, the body so exposed in its representational force, exposed, indeed, in its representational desire, is always susceptible to being read as the spectacularized body of the gay man" (208). In the past, nevertheless, the *Jefe* prevented such a reading of his body through the implicit threat of violence, and on one occasion, when Villena was looking at his exposed genitals, he smiled and said, "*Qué, ¿te gustan, eh?*" (72) [*What, you like them, huh?*], after which he turned Villena over his knee, pulled down his shorts and underwear, and gave him, "blandamente, unas cuantas azotainas" (72) [gently, a few lashings].

Because of his social background, Villena felt completely alienated within the camp setting. He was ignorant of the political content of the camp songs and jargon insofar as his family inhabited an altogether different world and disparaged what for them were the banalities of Francoist culture. To the amazement of his peers, he was visited daily by his grandmother's chauffeur, Plácido, who brought him special foods, cold drinks in crystal glasses, folding chairs and mattresses, and whatever other personal amenities he desired. Villena describes with camplike humor the incongruous figure that he must have cut in the eyes of the other boys — "La rareza que yo representaba en aquel lugar, con el chófer, la sombrilla y el pijama de seda" (75) [the oddity that I represented in that place, with my chauffeur, sun umbrella, and silk pajamas]. According to Babuscio, the humor of camp results specifically from this "incongruity between an object, person, or situation and its context" (26).

Eventually, the director of the camp requested to speak with Villena's grandmother, presumably to ask her to refrain from sending the child luxury items through the chauffeur and thereby disturbing the normal camp routine. During one of her visits, Villena informed her of the director's request, but she refused to let him even approach her. From Villena's adult perspective, her behavior represented the epitome of aristocratic performativity, which, though oppressive in its original context, was turned against the oppressiveness of contemporary fascist culture and used to silence the voice that silenced difference:

> La abuela me oyó en silencio, miró tras unas gafas de sol que llevaba en la mano al buen hombre que ya sonreía, y antes de hablar otra vez conmigo de nuestras cosas, le dijo seca y normalmente al chófer: *Plácido, adelántese, y dígale que no le recibo.* Obedeció el fámulo la orden, y el estupor del falangista debió de ser indecible. Pero no rechistó, y nunca volvió a decirme nada. Y supongo que no por servilismo, sino por lo extraño y mágico de aquella presencia señorial, arcaica y dignísima en un medio tan ajeno a ella y tan adverso. El viejo poder de la aristocracia, *la presencia lejana,* había funcionado de nuevo. El resto debía ser silencio. (77–78)

> [Grandmother listened to me in silence, looked through some sunglasses she was carrying in her hand at the good man who was now smiling, and before speaking again to me about our affairs, she said to the chauffeur in a brusque and normal voice: "Plácido, go over and tell him that I shan't receive him." The servant obeyed the order, and the astonishment of the Falangist must have been indescribable. But he didn't say a word, and he never again said anything to me. And I imagine that it was not on account of servility but the strangeness and magic of that seignorial presence, archaic and so dignified in an environment so alien to her and so adverse. The ancient power of the aristocracy, *the distant presence,* had worked again. The rest had to be silence.]

Ironically, this aristocratic power, which insulated the young Villena from the roughness and vulgarity of his companions, further distanced him from the masculine companionship he craved.

Despite his estrangement within the Francoist camp, Villena regarded summer as an idealized period of fulfillment. Most of his vacations were spent in Alicante, where, like Gil de Biedma in La Nava, he remembers "una casi inmutable sensación de plenitud, de calor, de luz, que se me hace difícil deslindar pues me aparece como bloque, como entidad sin fisuras, como tiempo sin transcurrir, es decir, mítico" (81) [an almost immutable sensation of plenitude, of warmth, of light, that I find difficult to demarcate since it appears to me like a block, like an entity without fissure, like time without passage, that is to say, mythical].[7] During one particular summer, this edenic bliss was broken when he became acutely aware of his nascent sexuality and of his profound separation from males of his own age. While taking an afternoon siesta at the country house of relatives, he heard a group of boys outside his room talking and laughing. He went to the window and discovered that they were discussing sex and touching each other's penises. Suddenly, he was overcome with a feeling of both envy and unnaturalness: "Lo que a mí, sobre todo, me llegó fue el calor, el aura, la fuerza telúrica de lo que allí, llanamente y sin misterio, sucedía. . . . Y sentí envidia. La terrible envidia de no ser tan natural como ellos" (87) [What reached me, above all, was the warmth, the aura, the telluric force of what there, openly and without mystery, was occurring. . . . And I felt envy. The terrible envy of not being as natural as they were]. Afterward, he consciously masturbated for the first time in his life, fantasizing not only the male body but an entire natural (masculine, heterosexual) world from which he was excluded.

The Denaturalization of the Natural

In the final section of *Ante el espejo,* "Reflejos" [Reflections], Villena exposes the workings of the natural/unnatural binary (which for him subsumes the masculine/feminine and heterosexual/homosexual binary oppositions) through a meditation on autobiographical prosopopeia and the vexed question of personal identity. Just as in childhood he stood before the mirror, assuming a multitude of poses and personalities, so in his memoir he admits having donned a mask. This mask, he maintains, like the make-believe roles of the past, is as genuine as anything that might lie behind it (129). Villena therefore comes to affirm a multiplicity of identities that he views as interrelated:

> El muchachito tímido que jugaba a ser estrella de cine, y el egiptólogo posterior que se imaginaba un sabio austero, y el decadente y lánguido que con corbata violeta soñaba encontrar también en Argelia algún mogrebí mocito con deseo paralelo de exotismo, lucimiento y sexo, en el fondo eran la misma persona. (131)

[The timid little boy who played at being a movie star, and the subsequent Egyptologist who imagined himself an austere wise man, and the decadent and languid one who with a violet tie dreamed also of finding in Algiers a little Arab lad with a similar desire for the exotic and for brilliance and for sex, deep down were the same person.][8]

This "same person," in spite of his numerous avatars, is a reflection of the dandy, the "señoritín finisecular ante el espejo" (132) [the *fin-de-siècle* little gentleman in the mirror]. As autobiographer, Villena has attempted to shed his dandyism. He declares in *Corsarios* that he is all but finished with it (163), and at the close of *Ante el espejo* he fancies a life of action free from the posturing and aesthetic distancing of the alienated, homosexual aristocrat. He imagines fleeing to a Polynesian island to live a life of sun and flesh or becoming an adventurer in Maracaibo who has never read a single book or a politician who fights for a noble cause or a singer of frivolous songs who leads a completely banal but extraordinary life (131). Yet though the roles have been rescripted and the scenarios altered, these narratives remain haunted by the childhood desire for the natural. Villena hence envisions the release of a natural self ("el primitivo que todos poseemos dentro" [132] [the primitive that we all have within]) and a repatriation to a primeval "south" that would become the site of the life that he was denied (132). This natural self is nonetheless an illusion (the primitive being the most incongruous and campiest of all the roles of the decadent dandy), and in the end the "same person" is not a particular character but the actor himself.

In striving to transcend the unnaturalness of his youth, Villena appropriates the myth of the natural (and with it the fundamental Euro-centric image of the exotic south),[9] but rather than merely replicating it, he reconfigures it in a way that ultimately reveals its constructedness. The protagonists of his childhood and adult narratives are no more than actors, and each performance is continually supplanted by a new one in an unending quest for a natural identity that is itself always other, insofar as identity, according to the logic of hetero-relationality, is not self-sufficient but internally mediated by what it is not. Villena is unable to achieve a natural (heterosexual and masculine) identity because heterosexual masculinity is itself riven by its unnatural (homosexual and feminine) contrary. What is more, when Villena posits the other as natural, he does so in reference to his own "unnaturalness," transforming him, through a Midaslike touch that drains its object of its natural essence, into the "non non-natural," and thereby establishing a pattern of infinite regress, or mirrors. It is in this contradiction that Villena discerns the failure of love:

> Porque — finalmente — nadie estamos de acuerdo con el que somos ni con el que hemos sido. Necesitamos siempre lo que está *más allá.* El amor que está siempre en *el otro,* y luego en el otro aún más lejos y más arriba, y el otro que no somos y que dejaríamos atrás también si llegáramos a serlo. ¡Permanente atracción de lo que está enfrente y a distancia! (132)

> [Because in the final analysis none of us is in agreement with what we are or what we have been. We always need what is *beyond.* The love that is always in *the other,* and then in the other even farther ahead and farther up, and the other that we are not and that we would leave behind if we were to become him. Permanent attraction of what is in front of us and at a distance!]

The loved one for Villena is thus like a mirage on an ever-receding horizon of ontological selfhood.

In the last scene of *Ante el espejo* Villena even undermines his role as writer (and in so doing the master narrative of all literary autobiography) through a camp foretelling of his future as an elderly and jaded man of letters. He pictures himself on the terrace of a seaside hotel, in a state of semi-inebriation, advising a young man to give up writing and live for the moment while simultaneously dispensing money to two young gigolos. In this scenario, he maintains his original role as poseur by denying the seriousness of literature and love and by playing the part of the "aging homosexual." He is thus finally relieved of the myth of naturalness and remains consistent with his own inherent artificiality:

> el niño que hacía poses ante el espejo, con corbata ancha y manos de paje con sortijas, habrá triunfado, y habrá sido coherente consigo mismo: vivir siempre en la intensidad, ya que tal vez nunca es posible huir ni ser el anhelado *otro,* el absoluto diferente. (132–33)

> [the child who posed before the mirror, with a wide tie and the hands of a page with rings, will have triumphed and will have remained coherent with himself: to live always intensely, since it is perhaps never possible to flee nor to be the longed-for *other,* the absolute different.]

In the end, then, authenticity is to be found not in the object of difference but in the execution of the theatrical gesture itself.[10]

Villena carries his anti-essentialism to its ultimate conclusion, rejecting a fixed personal identity as well as the entire transcendental foundation of human reality.[11] He does this not through the production of an original discourse of his own (now no longer possible in the wake of egological dispossession), but through a "piggybacking" (Meyer 11) on other poetic voices which, in the context of his completed memoir, take on a new and different meaning. He cites the poet Khayyám: "*Todo esto es tan sólo un puñado de polvo bajo el soplo del viento*" (133) [All this is but a handful of dust beneath the blowing of the wind]. In this passage unity (the whole within the all-encompassing hand) is reduced to multiplicity and detached from its social and divine moorings. In the last sentence, an echo of San Juan de la Cruz, this dust becomes an intuition of death and annihilation: "Milésimas de polvo en la noche oscura y giratoria de un vacío tremendo" (133) [Thousands of particles of dust in the dark and swirling night of a tremendous void]. Like the actor's makeup, and the detritus of the human body itself, it is all that will remain in the aftermath of a lifetime of performance.

Terenci Moix

Looking Queer

When Terenci Moix was fourteen years old, he first witnessed an act of civil disobedience. As he was about to purchase a copy of *La Vanguardia* from a kiosk on the Paralelo of Barcelona, a throng of Catalán dissidents suddenly burst down the street, shouting and seizing newspapers. At the time, he was completely unaware of the historical significance of the incident, and as the police began to club and arrest the protesters, he felt a profound sense of relief. And with good reason too. After all, poor Norma Shearer had been led off to the guillotine by a similar sort of mob in the film *Marie Antoinette*. According to his autobiographical volumes, *El cine de los sábados* [The Saturday matinee] and *El beso de Peter Pan* [The kiss of Peter Pan], Hollywood cinema (and to a lesser degree radio, comics, and film in general) determined his childhood vision of the world and himself and constituted him as "la perfecta imagen del jovencito colonizado" (299) [the perfect image of the colonized little lad].[1] This cinematic colonization preceded his birth (his mother supposedly went into labor during a screening of *Gaslight*), fixing the parameters of his alienation as a gay youth while simultaneously establishing the context for his eventual act of defiance as an openly gay writer and autobiographer. For the young Moix, however, cinema was not simply an instrument of social control (or "mass culture," as propounded by the Frankfurt School), but rather, as Michael Denning writes with regard to the term "popular culture," "a contested terrain" (253). During his formative years Moix in fact both passively internalized and, through the prism of his burgeoning homoerotic desire, actively refocused the heterosexual (and heterosexist) lens of Hollywood cinema. As Frances Wyers writes of the collaborative efforts of the readers of *El beso de la mujer araña,* he ultimately "retrieves and refashions works made for indoctrination and manipulation" (181). His autobiography thus offers insight into the interconnectedness of popular culture and gay self-representation, positing gay sexuality not as an essence but as a gaze through which the ostensibly natural constructions of heterosexual ideology are denaturalized and rendered queer.

Hollywood Cinema and the Queer Gaze

Gaze theory, as advanced by film scholars, has for the most part been grounded in gender (as opposed to the power structures of Foucauldian analysis) and articulated through the psychoanalytic paradigms of Freud and Lacan. In the 1975 landmark essay "Visual Pleasure and Narrative Cinema," Laura Mulvey set the terms of debate for a whole generation of psychoanalytic film critics by arguing that Hollywood cinema aims precisely to satisfy the unconscious desire of heterosexual males. Though she allowed for female pleasure through identification with the male perspective, Mulvey remained focused on how cinematic narrative structures the experience of the spectator. More recent film theorists, while often retaining the psychoanalytic framework of Mulvey, have attempted to address lesbian and gay male spectatorship through a reexamination and reconfiguration of spectator agency. Steven Drukman, for example, delineates a formula for a gay male gaze whereby "the object of scopophilic pleasure is the man and the subject of ego-identification is . . . in constant flux between the woman and the man" (84–85).[2] Whereas such a distinction destabilizes the position of the viewer and loosens the gaze from the gridlock of monolithic gender identities, the object of desire remains fixed. In contrast to Drukman's "gay gaze," a "queer gaze" might be said to subvert the identities of not only the spectators but their objects as well. As Caroline Evans and Lorraine Gamman suggest, it might even challenge the essentialist idea that "relations of looking are determined by the biological sex of the individual/s you choose to fornicate with, more than any other social relations (such as those associated with ethnic or class subjectivities)" (40).

In elucidating the theory of homographesis, Lee Edelman situates the discussion of the gaze and cinematic spectatorship in a historical context, noting the intriguing fact that modern homosexuality, as articulated in late-nineteenth-century medical and legal treatises, and the technology capable of making cinema a major cultural force were both produced at the same moment in the development of industrial capitalism (200). The early discourses of homosexuality, like the patriarchal ideology operative in traditional, mainstream films, sought to affirm heterosexual masculinity as the universal male nature by representing the male homosexual as psychologically and socially deviant. Yet cinema as a medium implicitly questions the naturalness of heterosexual masculinity by reversing "the culturally determined meanings and relations of looking and being looked at" (Edelman 200). Through film, the male body is given as an object to be seen. What is more, masculinity is transformed from a supposed essence into an appearance to the extent that it is performed. Steven Cohan and Ina Rae Hark thus write: "The male's seeming exemption from visual representation may work very hard to preserve the cultural fiction that masculinity is not a social construction, but American movies have always served as one of the primary sites through which the culture, in the process of promulgating that fiction, has also exposed its workings as a mythology" (3). As Hark further clarifies, the spectacularization of the male is frequently coded in films as unnatural (152). Cinema nevertheless remains a site where the constructedness of gender identity is made explicit.

The notion of a natural masculinity, that simply is and need not appear in order to be, is destabilized through the act of representation fundamental to all the performing arts. This destabilization is intensified by a feminization as well as an overmasculinization of the male role. As Lacan contends, "In the human being, virile display itself appears as feminine" (85; qtd. in Edelman 208). Gay and lesbian actors, moreover, frequently leave a mark on the cinematic product (Dyer, "Entertainment" 278); and the masculine posturing of such performers as James Dean in *Giant* is so highly stylized that it becomes a camp parody of masculinity (Dyer, "Rock" 28). Not only is masculine identity performed in popular cinema, but when posited as an object of desire through the gaze of a gay male viewer, the subject/object binary of the ostensibly masculine heterosexual character and feminine homosexual viewer is inverted. It is through cinema viewing that homoerotic desire is in fact often articulated. Edelman writes: "The cinema affords the gay male spectator an opportunity to focus on the issue of bodiliness and ways of wearing the body precisely because the image on the screen is disembodied and fragmented. It allows, that is, for the intense scrutiny of the body as such — and from close up — without fear of being seen in the guilty enterprise of looking" (271n21). As Judith Mayne urges us to remember, however, this " 'safe zone' in which homosexual as well as heterosexual desires can be fantasized and acted out" is not indicative of "an innate capacity to 'read against the grain,' but rather of the way in which desire and pleasure in the cinema may well function to problematize the categories of heterosexual versus homosexual" (97).

According to *El beso de Peter Pan,* the adolescent Ramón[3] experienced concrete, erotic desire while watching performances by Steve Reeves and other male actors. He furthermore attempted to emulate what he perceived to be gay-inclined males in such characters as Carl Trask, played by James Dean in *East of Eden* (141). After seeing this particular film, he openly declared his hatred for his father, whose ritual remark at Sunday dinner, "Preferiría tener un hijo muerto antes que maricón" (142) [I would rather have a dead son than a queer one], revealed to him the latent violence of heterosexual patriarchy.[4] Ironically, though not surprisingly, it was through the overtly heterosexist cinema of Hollywood, imposed on Spain by the cultural colonialism of the United States, that he managed to resist indigenous heterosexism. As Dyer points out, several major American actors of the 1950s, including James Dean, Montgomery Clift, and Sal Mineo, were not only "to some degree or other, gay," but "fit a certain stereotype of the gay man — sad, neurotic, confused, . . . physically slight, with intense eyes and pretty faces" ("Rock" 28); and along with Tony Curtis, Tab Hunter, and Marlon Brando, they formed part of the gay iconography of the period.[5] In one piece of youthful writing Ramón even imagines starring in a film as the son of Rock Hudson in a script written expressly for the two of them by John Steinbeck. He thereby establishes a symbolic connection with a real gay man through and in spite of his heterosexual representation on the screen. While this might be taken as an affirmation on his part of a transnational and transcultural gay male identity, what his text demonstrates, as Mayne writes with regard to lesbian and gay spectatorship in general, is "how going to the movies *situates* gay/lesbian desire in specific ways" (166; emphasis added).

Peter Pan Moix: Lost Boy and Fairy

Moix makes much of the fact that crucial events of his life, including the beginning of his mother's labor and his own first sexual encounter, actually took place in movie houses. He maintains that his personal identity (and specifically his sexuality) is inseparable from the images he saw projected on the screen during childhood and adolescence. In analyzing the first volume of memoirs, *El cine de los sábados,* Smith thus writes that for Moix "desire must be projected before it can be felt (and projected on to the widest possible screen)" (*Laws* 48). He further clarifies that to the extent that Moix conceives of the self as fundamentally cinematic, and hence as flat, he avoids the probing of identity and of a tormented sexuality so typical of traditional gay autobiographers. It is Smith's contention that "if the limits of the cinema screen are identical with those of the world (if subjectivity is a purely aesthetic category), then there can remain no ground at all on which to take up an ethical position" (*Laws* 52). In *El beso de Peter Pan,* nevertheless, Moix begins to stake out such a space. He continues to view himself as a product of cinematic culture, yet he specifically re-represents the film narratives of his youth, the most significant of which is *Peter Pan.* In so doing he does not posit an inherently gay identity but contests the ideology of identity on which heterosexual hegemony is founded. *El beso de Peter Pan* is therefore a moral and political gesture. As the opening scene reveals, it is also a fairy tale of gay male love.

> Cuando Peter Pan me besó en una pérgola de los jardines de Nunca Jamás tuve miedo de que su amor fuese flor de un día y decidí apropiarme de su puñal para obligarle a recurrir a mí en momentos de peligro. Pero el héroe me aseguró que tal precaución era innecesaria porque nunca nos separaríamos. A guisa de confirmación nos hicimos unos cortes en las muñecas y mezclamos nuestra sangre y por eso conozco que por mis venas corre el polvillo de estrellas que sólo tienen los niños eternos. (29)

[When Peter Pan kissed me in a pergola of the gardens of Never Land, I was afraid that his love might be a one-day flower, and I decided to seize his dagger in order to force him to return to me in moments of danger. But the hero assured me that such a precaution was unnecessary because we would never be parted. By way of confirmation we made cuts in our wrists and mixed our blood and therefore I know that through my veins flows the star dust that only eternal children have.]

In this passage Moix rescripts the conventional Peter Pan narrative. Whereas in most renditions Peter avoids his sexuality, preferring, for example, that Wendy play the part of little mother instead of mistress or wife, in *El beso de Peter Pan* he makes his initial appearance as a lover, and a gay one at that. In keeping with the masculinity of the Walt Disney character, he comes equipped with a weapon of violence.[6] At the outset Ramón is passive — the image of masculinity emerges from the screen and awakens him with a kiss. Yet when this Sleeping Beauty comes to life, he attempts to take control of his situation, going first for the knife — and years later for the autobiographer's pen. What he seeks is not only love but also safety from violence. To achieve it, he must appropriate the phallic weapon (and with it the heterosexist apparatus of Hollywood cinema) and convert it into an instrument of male reciprocity. Ramón and Peter consequently engage in an act of blood brotherhood, but rather than blood itself, it is the star dust of the dream factory that constitutes their commonality.[7] This ersatz essence binds Ramón to the dominant culture of Hollywood while instilling in him the illusion that he might fly away like a fairy. In re-representing the Peter Pan movie, Moix thus highlights its intrinsic fakeness, and in the process de-essentializes both his own and Peter's sexuality through a camp performance whose ultimate aim is freedom.

Though Ramón occasionally engages in "camp behavior" by explicitly imitating the feminine, he is more apt to adopt Meyer's "camp eye" or what Dyer calls a "camp attitude" (42) vis-à-vis the dominant culture. Dyer elucidates the concept "camp attitude": "There is a difference between camp behaviour and a camp attitude. The latter implies an ironic stance towards official or mainstream images or representations. Camp in this sense is profoundly denaturalizing. Far from expressing a sense of what is natural, it constantly draws attention to the artifices attendant on the construction of images of what is natural" (*The Matter of Images* 42). Drukman makes this point more subtle by arguing that camp is not the same as the gay gaze, but instead is "a primary hue through which the gay gaze is filtered" (87). As such it is an instrument that helps recast the subject/object binary of hetero-relationality and that lightens the dynamic of scopophilia altogether: "Like a rose-tinted pair of glasses kept in the breast pocket of the gay male specta-tor, camp is ever handy, but used more for cosmetic reasons than for clarity of vision. In other words, camp allows for a more seamless shifting (between object of scopophilia and subject of ego-identification) for the gay gaze. Rose-tinted lenses blur the rigid constraints of 'straight' heterosexual narra-tive, making it easier on the eyes" (88).

In camping *Peter Pan,* Moix actually seizes on ambiguities already pres-ent in the original text. Peter is in fact an androgynous character, usually played by a woman and distinguished by what Jacqueline Rose describes as a "swaggering effeminacy" (xiii). He first appeared in J. M. Barrie's *The Little White Bird,* which according to Rose is charged with the erotic desire of a man for a little boy. Subsequent theatrical and cinematic productions of the Peter Pan narrative have endeavored "to wipe out the residual signs of the disturbance out of which it was produced" (5).[8] Yet an "unsettling of gender identities" (xiii) remains, and in a 1991 version staged at London's Drill Hall, Peter is played as a lesbian in disguise (ix), and the famous call for audience participation — "clap your hands if you believe in fairies" — is cast in an ex-plicitly queer context (xiii). Moix's reading of Peter draws specifically on the paradox of "a little boy who flies away because he does not want to grow up" (26), that is, a child who must abandon the protective sphere of the child-hood nursery (and in the process steal other children) in order to remain an eternal child. As a youth, Ramón himself inhabits a hostile world (better a dead son than a queer one), and his escape involves an effort not only to re-tain his childhood identity but also to forge a refuge from an alien adult soci-ety. The space for this refuge is provided by Hollywood, but unlike the Never Land of Disney and of most previous adaptations of *Peter Pan,* his enchanted isle of lost boys and fairies is imagined as a distinctively homo-erotic utopia.

As Dyer maintains, the Hollywood construction of utopia is clearly a problematical enterprise, since "to draw attention to the gap between what is and what could be, is, ideologically speaking, playing with fire" ("Enter-tainment" 279). Although most mainstream Hollywood productions try to work through the contradictions raised by utopian representations "in such a way as to 'manage' them, to make them seem to disappear[,] [t]hey don't always succeed" (279). This is clearly the case with Never Land. Through the use of temporal negation, Never Land is posited as a place without time.[9] It is dehistoricized, like the mythical child of the adult imagination or, for that matter, lesbian and gay culture in general under patriarchy. For Ramón, however, it is also the realm of a boy unlike any other boy, who excites his homoerotic desire while holding forth the promise of an idyllic space in which love between men is possible. For this reason his Never Land is not a static and timeless entity but the site on which sexuality is produced and homo-praxis temporalized.

That notwithstanding, Ramón's first real sexual encounter, which occurs in the Cine Cervantes of Barcelona during a screening of the film version of *Aïda* with Sophia Loren, is altogether different from the imaginary affair with Peter Pan depicted at the outset of *El beso de Peter Pan*. As the scene of jealousy between Aïda and Amneris unfolds, Ramón feels a hand unzip his pants and begin to masturbate him. He continues to sit passively with his eyes riveted to the screen, and in the moment of climax witnesses a subliminal penetration as the victorious soldiers of Radamés, having returned from the Nubian campaign, make their triumphal entry into the city of Memphis. From his adult perspective, the cacophony of emotions experienced in the moment ("placer," "necesidad urgente de llorar," "voluntad de echar a correr, de liberarme y al mismo tiempo de sucumbir" [100] [pleasure, urgent need to cry, desire to start running, to free myself and at the same time to succumb]) are overshadowed and enveloped by the absurd artificiality of the film:

No podía pedirse mayor acumulación de falsedades: Sofía Loren embetunada para parecer princesa etíope y expresando sus cuitas con la voz prestada de la Tebaldi, mientras la Simionato cedía la suya a Lois Maxwell, disfrazada de hija de los faraones sin anunciar que, con los años, acabaría haciendo de permanente secretaria de James Bond. (101)

[One could not ask for a greater accumulation of falsities: Sophia Loren in black-face in order to look like an Ethiopian princess and telling her troubles with the dubbed voice of Tebaldi, while Simionato relinquished hers to Lois Maxwell, disguised as the daughter of the pharaohs, without revealing that over the years she would end up playing the permanent secretary of James Bond.]

ung Ramón nevertheless sees himself diametrically opposed to the
_____ f *Aïda*. Whereas they appear endowed with glamorous bodies and
grand passions, he is an awkward and unattractive adolescent being fondled
by a middle-aged man. His drama, moreover, takes place in silence and dark-
ness, and though he might turn to face the figure at his side, he remains
transfixed by the overarching narrative of *Aïda*. As autobiographer Moix exposes both the unnaturalness of the film as well as the incongruity of the
events on the screen and in the darkened rows of a cinema called Cervantes:
"más adelante encontré divertido contar que la primera vez que me metieron
mano fue en un cine con nombre de escritor manco" (101) [later I found it
amusing to tell that the first time someone put his hand in my pants was in a
theater named after a one-handed writer]. In rereading the episode he hence
conflates both "low" (popular cinematic) and "high" (operatic and, by im-
plication, Cervantine) culture.[10] More important, he makes the public space
of cultural representation (the movie house as opposed to the private sphere
of the "closet") the locus of the expression of a marginalized sexuality. As an
adolescent, Ramón attempts to escape the homoeroticism of the Cine Cervantes by running out the door of the theater. Eventually, however, he
achieves a veritable "coming out" when he learns to perform his sexuality as
a "counter-act" to the dominant representations he observes.

Although Ramón initially flees the world of gay sexuality, several gay
males play a decisive role in his adolescent development. The most influen-
tial of these is Roberto.[11] As competing members of an acting school, they
first see each other as rivals, but a friendship develops when they accidentally
meet at a screening of *Ben-Hur*. Although Ramón remained alienated from
his sexual partner in the Cine Cervantes, he and Roberto manage to dissociate themselves from the discourse of the film and establish a complicity as
gay viewers. Roberto initiates the operation through ironic comments and
gestures. Ramón responds with uncontrollable laughter:

A mi lado, Roberto tenía el rostro exacto de la inocencia. Su fingida gravedad
acentuaba mi diversión mientras la altisonante música de Miklos Rosza pro-
clamaba que nos hallábamos ante un momento sublime de la historia de la hu-
manidad. Acababa de nacer el Mesías. Lástima que yo no paraba de reír. (338)

[At my side, Roberto had the perfect face of innocence. His feigned seriousness accentuated my amusement while the high-sounding music of

Miklos Rosza proclaimed that we were witnessing a sublime moment in the history of humanity. The Messiah had just been born. Too bad I couldn't stop laughing.]

In this way Ramón mocks the aesthetics of the film as well as the values that it professes. He laughs at the representation of the Nativity, thereby rejecting the official religion of his culture and expressing delight at the "advent" of Roberto in his life and the "birth" of their friendship. Through an act of play, he and Roberto thus achieve a temporary space of their own within the domain of the movie house and in opposition to the representation on the screen.[12]

At the conclusion of *Ben-Hur,* as Roberto and Ramón leave the cinema, Roberto begins to question the ostensible heterosexuality of the characters Ben-Hur and Messala and argues that the two are actually bound by a homo-erotic passion. Ramón is caught off guard by his argument and insists that the meaning of their relationship is to be found in the conflict between Jew-ish nationalism and Roman imperialism. Yet according to Roberto, they are lovers: "Por eso le da a Mesala esa rabieta. . . . A nadie le da una rabieta tan gorda por cosas del nacionalismo ese. Tiene que haber una pasión" (340) [That's why Messala has that fit . . . No one throws such a hissy fit because of that nationalism stuff. There has to be passion]. He further contends that essential scenes of love between Ben-Hur and Messala have been cut and that as it stands, the film makes no sense.[13] In reading the film in this way, Roberto not only indulges in a homoerotic fantasy but also reveals an intu-ition of how heterosexuality and homosexuality are interconnected and how an affirmation of the former is predicated on and even requires an im-plicit affirmation of the latter.

Ramón and Roberto become inseparable friends, and Roberto eventually suggests that they imitate the relationship of Messala and Ben-Hur as he has interpreted it. Although Ramón is cognizant of his own homoerotic desire, he tries at this point to assert a heterosexual identity, and when Roberto an-nounces that he will willingly adopt a feminine role in order to comply with Ramón's feigned machismo, the latter ascribes to him the negative stereo-type of "las maricas más detestadas" (380) [the most detested little fag-gots]. Ironically, whereas Roberto strives to rescript the heterosexist cinema of Hollywood and in so doing create a positive gay relationship, Ramón unwittingly plays the part of censor, restraining his homoerotic desire and rigorously enforcing the literal interpretation of the cinematic fictions that dominated his early years. Soon afterward, he admits to himself his desire for Roberto, but before he can win him back, Roberto takes a different lover. As a consequence, Ramón experiences a nervous collapse. His mother sends him to a psychiatrist, who treats him with disgust and contempt, as well as to a series of faith healers, all of whom fail to "cure" him of his homosexuality or relieve him of his psychological and physical malaise. Only gradually does he recover from the loss of Roberto as a lover (the two actually remain friends for years, until the latter's death from AIDS), realizing that his unhappiness resulted not from his sexual desire per se, but from his inability to rescript his life in accordance with Roberto's queer reading of the movies.

As autobiographer, Moix in fact comes to blame Peter Pan for Ramón's failed relationship with Roberto (412). Though Peter continues to elicit Ramón's homoerotic desire, he actually holds him captive, charming him with seductive images but obstructing reciprocity with real boys his age — "los niños que Peter Pan ató a la butaca de un cine de barrio para que se les llenasen los ojos con imágenes destinadas a no abandonarles jamás" (416) [the boys that Peter Pan tied to the seat of a neighborhood cinema in order to fill their eyes with images destined never to abandon them]. Peter haunts Ramón's every fantasy, appearing in the guises of lover, friend, and even progenitor, and in the end subsuming the entire secondhand repertoire of popular imagery that Ramón recycles in order to reproduce himself. In nightly rituals of masturbation, he conjures forth images of Peter, whose kiss leaves on his lips a wound "que sólo otros labios más maduros podrían cerrar" (390) [that only other more mature lips could heal]. As a result, his homoerotic desire short-circuits, and all that remains is the debris of Hollywood. In a particularly graphic passage Moix depicts his childhood persona as "el último aborto de las brujas que, en un aquelarre insensato, jodieron con Peter Pan" (303) [the final abortion of the witches who, in a senseless witches' sabbath, screwed with Peter Pan]. The agent here is of course Ramón himself in the vortex of his fantasies. What is significant is that in each of his avatars, Peter Pan continues to reveal a homoeroticism representative of Ramón's sexuality. Moix finally suggests that Ramón and Peter are one and the same ("acaso [su] beso fuese el mío propio" [390] [perhaps his kiss was my very own]), and as imaginary gay clones Ramón carries the blood of Peter

Pan not only in his veins but "hasta el fondo de su ano" (454) [to the end of his anus]. Ultimately, however, "Peter Pan Moix" disappears when the young adult fully expresses his sexuality. For this reason the child eludes the mature life writer as the impossible other of all autobiographical praxis.

Si(gh)ting Never Land

In the "Epílogo en Nunca Jamás" [Epilogue in Never Land] that follows the narration of adolescence, Moix orchestrates a complex scenario in which the adult autobiographer (Terenci) confronts the figures of Peter Pan, Ramón, and the alter ego that he has attempted to forge throughout his writing career. This latter persona, El Niño del Invierno [the Winter Boy], first appears in the prologue to *El beso de Peter Pan,* as Terenci visits the site in Paris (the second floor of a bookshop inhabited by expatriate youth) where his final transition from childhood to adulthood occurred in what he describes as the glorious year of 1963. El Niño del Invierno is identified with winter to the extent that the youthful Moix sought to escape the fullness of life through his cultivation of the imaginary. Yet he is not the Ramón of the past, but is instead a product of the writer's imagination and, along with Terenci, a fictional representation of the writing-self. Whereas El Niño del Invierno is implicitly present whenever Moix reflects on the past, Ramón remains inaccessible, not only because he has ceased to exist, but also because his existence was ultimately articulated through a fantasy that the adult can no longer sustain.

Moix writes that one day while in Paris, Ramón attends a screening of the film *All about Eve* (which he describes as "el apasionamiento de los cinéfilos y el delirio de las mariquitas adeptas al culto de Bette" [471–72] [the passion of cinephiles and the rapture of the little fairies that followed the cult of Bette]), and as he is leaving the cinema of Chaillot, whom should he encounter but El Niño Eterno [the Eternal Boy], Peter Pan. The two initiate an animated discussion of the movie. Peter criticizes its aesthetics, and Ramón wonders if he has turned Marxist: "Sólo faltaría que se arrancara con un discurso sobre Brecht o Piscator. Pero no eran aquéllas sus intenciones. Por el contrario, estaba en onda de seductor" (472) [The only thing left was for him to break into a speech on Brecht or Piscator. But those weren't his intentions. On the contrary, he was out to pick someone up]. Ramón agrees to his overtures, if only to convince him that Mankiewicz is a great director. (As with Roberto, a homoerotic relationship is constructed in reference to a mainstream Hollywood film.) When they reach the bookshop where he sleeps, Ramón shows Peter an old edition of the work of J. M. Barrie, whom Peter labels "puritan" for having failed to tell the truth about his relationship with Captain Hook and the displeasure the latter felt when Peter chose to escape to Shangri-la with Kim of India. His was in fact a tale of homoerotic love, as Roberto knew to be the case with *Ben-Hur.* Before Peter and Ramón ascend to the upstairs room, the fairy tale is thus revealed as such.[14]

When they reach the next floor, however, an unexpected visitor awaits them: El Niño del Invierno. In a sense this is the moment when the narrative of the past is completed and childhood ends. Peter informs Ramón that El Niño del Invierno is not yet born, since some ten years will elapse before Moix begins to create him through his writing. Then Terenci himself enters, and he and Ramón gaze into each other's eyes. Again it is Peter who clarifies for Ramón the identity of the new visitor: "Ese tío eres tú" (475) [That guy's you]. Ramón is saddened by the vision of what he will become, and rather than merge with his image, he refuses the implicit narcissism of the adult autobiographer and pleads with Peter to take him away. Suddenly, "Peter Pan levantaba el vuelo, con el joven Ramón aferrado a sus muslos" (475) [Peter Pan took flight with the young Ramón clinging to his thighs], and the two fly off over the rooftops of Paris, carrying with them the entire cast of actors and characters that populated Moix's youth, including Michael Strogoff, the Little Lord, the body of Steve Reeves, and the face of Lillian Gish. Afterward, Terenci remains alone with El Niño del Invierno, pondering the past that he has managed to evoke throughout his writing but whose freshness and insolence ("el descaro primordial que fue el verdadero origen de la vida" [476] [the primordial effrontery that was the true origin of life]) he has failed to recover.

Moix's closing comments function as a gloss to the epilogue but leave unresolved the ambiguity of his quadripartite self-representation, which ultimately finds meaning in the spatial configuration of the scenario. Two interior spaces are posited — the cinema and the bookshop. These are the physical sites wherein culture is represented and where Ramón performs the primary activities (watching and reading) out of which his childhood self is constituted. Ramón is made by what he sees and reads, but through it (and specifically through the image of Peter Pan) he also attempts to make himself. The inevitable conflict (between Ramón and Peter and in the final analysis between Ramón and himself as both a passive and active agent of identity) is temporarily suspended when a third space is delineated in the intermediate zone separating the cinema from the bookshop. In the opening sentence of the epilogue Moix writes: "Ramón Moix Meseguer descubrió su juventud en uno de esos *quais* de París" (463) [Ramón Moix Meseguer discovered his youth on one of those quays of Paris]. This discovery occurs within neither the movie house nor the bookshop but outside, on the streets of the city and at the edge of the river. To accomplish it, Ramón must first "come out" of the cinema and assume his sexuality. (On previous occasions such a move involved a flight from his sexuality, as in the Cine Cervantes episode and even with Roberto.) As he and Peter make their way through the open space of the city, they themselves begin to project their images — "continuaron conversando por las viejas calles, reflejándose en los charcos de la lluvia reciente" (473) [they continued talking through the old streets, casting their reflection in the puddles from the recent rain]. Through the repetition of their steps, moreover, they actually stretch space out ("paseando, paseando" [473] [walking, walking]), increasing their distance from the cinema and the bookshop and momentarily transforming their marginal social position into a point of centrality. When they arrive at the quay beneath the bookshop, Peter "quiso detenerse junto al Sena para contemplar el reflejo de Notre Dame en sus aguas cabrilleantes" (473) [wanted to stop next to the Seine so as to contemplate the reflection of Notre Dame in its twinkling waters], but in response "Ramón le dijo que la iglesia se veía mucho mejor desde el sofá situado junto a la ventana" (473) [Ramón told him that the church could be seen much better from the sofa next to the window]. Through this decisive statement, Ramón "picks up" Peter Pan. Though as a result the child will presently be "picked up" and carried away forever, Ramón clearly becomes the agent of seduction of the companion at his side. He then takes him, via the bookshelves on the first floor, to the sofa in a corner of the upstairs room, which he claims as his "absoluta propiedad" (473) [absolute property]. In reaching this goal a long trajectory is completed, not only from the cinema of Chaillot through the streets of Paris, but also from that more distant movie house in Barcelona where his mother's labor first began, across the years of childhood and adolescence. Now it is he who waves his wand over Never Land, breathing new life into the lost boys and fairies of the enchanted isle. Perhaps in this moment he "makes love" for the first time to a real man, dispelling the child and his imaginary lover and living once and for all the youth he was denied and that he denied himself.[15] Perhaps he fancies himself free at last from the idols of the imagination and capable of forging his own destiny in the world. In either case, however, he remains bound to the text—whether as Ramón, El Niño del Invierno, Terenci, or Peter Pan himself, and the seeming rupture that occurs in the epilogue between child and adult, text and life, and cinema and self (in spatial terms the opening of an intermediate zone as the locus of freedom) is itself a fiction. As Moix has earlier admitted, he is not the author of his life, and in opposition to the realist illusion, he declares: "En literatura, como en la vida, el protagonista nace, pero no se hace" (294) [In literature, as in life, the protagonist is born, but he doesn't make himself].

Despite the dream of freedom, the autobiographical persona in all his incarnations remains overdetermined by the discourse of film. At one point death appears as the real through which the kaleidoscopic imagery of life will eventually be darkened and consumed. But death is also articulated through movie scripts. In meditating on the passing of family and friends Moix evokes the quintessential representation of the Grim Reaper ("empuñando la guadaña y el reloj de arena" [444] [brandishing the scythe and the hourglass]) from the final scene of Bergman's *The Seventh Seal,* envisioning himself as a latter-day Blanche Du Bois in the age of AIDS, dependent for solace on "la amabilidad de [sus] cadáveres" (439) [the kindness of his cadavers]. Even AIDS is a means of enacting a previously scripted identity, and in recalling the death of Gil de Biedma, Moix goes so far as to transform the disease into a final gesture of camp performance: "Se iría al otro mundo reteniendo como letanía última la inmortal proclama: «He necesitado muchos hombres en mi vida para llamarme Shanghai Lili»" (439) [He would depart for the other world keeping as his ultimate litany the immortal proclamation: "I have needed many men in my life in order to call myself Shanghai Lili"]. He thus continues to transcribe the cinematic texts through which his world has been mediated. He does not create images (as Rose has demonstrated in the case of Peter Pan, it is unlikely that any individual actually does) but instead casts his gaze on the ready-made images of his cultural milieu. In so doing he refocuses them, constituting himself not as the hero (Peter Pan Moix after all disappears before the end of the performance) but as a lens through which the imaginary is reorganized and re-represented. *El beso de Peter Pan* is therefore bound to its culture, but, like little Ramón dangling from the legs of Peter Pan, the text deflects its course, revealing an alternate perspective on the world and in the process rendering the image of Moix's own experience as a gay adolescent in postwar Francoist Spain.

CHAPTER SIX

Pedro Almodóvar

The Drag of Writing One's Life

The writing of Pedro Almodóvar, like much of his more extensive film corpus, reveals a series of discursive tensions present in numerous gay autobiographies.[1] In the course of his career, however, and especially after the production of the 1987 film *La ley del deseo* [The law of desire], he progressively distances himself from the paradigms of gay essentialism. Smith speaks of Almodóvar's "increasing disavowal of homosexuality, whether it is understood as a cultural identity, a recognizable sensibility, or a specific filmic tradition" (*Laws* 164); and in an interview for the gay and lesbian news magazine *The Advocate,* Almodóvar states: "I may be gay, but my films are not" (qtd. in Murphy 40). Despite what James Mandrell calls his "professional latent heterosexuality" (43), Almodóvar nevertheless continues to queer dominant configurations of sexuality through the dynamics of camp.[2] In his single book-length publication, *Patty Diphusa y otros textos* [*Patty Diphusa and Other Writings*], this queering is coupled with an explicit act of self-representation. Edited in 1991, *Patty Diphusa y otros textos* contains the memoirs of the fictional Patty Diphusa, a character that first appeared in the 1982 film *Laberinto de pasiones* [Labyrinth of passions].[3] Though originally issued in serial form between 1983 and 1984, the Patty Diphusa memoirs are followed in the 1991 text by short stories and essays from the middle and late 1980s. Throughout these pieces Almodóvar weaves his own autobiographical persona. What is more, he performs an aesthetic and ontological reversal according to which "la realidad imita al porno" (21) [reality imitates porno (9)]. In fact Almodóvar not only writes himself through the medium of a quasi-pornography but even queers this most problematical and contested of popular genres by allowing the object of the pornographic gaze to assert, at least tentatively, a subject position vis-à-vis the agents of its rhetorical alterity. In so doing he makes manifest both the possibilities and limitations of a radical camp praxis.

When Camp Goes All the Way

As John Ellis writes, pornography is not "an inherent attribute of certain representations" but "rather a designation given to a class of representations which is defined by particular ideological currents active in our society" (146). According to the British "Williams Report" (the Report of the Committee on Obscenity and Film Censorship) made during the late 1970s, pornography possesses two fundamental characteristics: "It has a certain function or intention, to arouse its audience sexually, and also has a certain content, explicit representations of sexual material. . . . A work has to have both this function and this content to be a piece of pornography" (qtd. in Ellis 153). In keeping with this standard definition (which not only raises the thorny question of intentionality but also erases the gender of both the viewers and the bodies viewed), the Patty Diphusa narrative is clearly not pornographic. The journal in which the Patty Diphusa series originally appeared, *La Luna de Madrid,* was similar to Andy Warhol's *Interview,* and its readers were undoubtedly more varied than the largely heterosexual male audience toward which most mass-produced pornography is directed. Although several passages of *Patty Diphusa* depict heterosexual acts, it is unlikely that Almodóvar wrote them primarily to arouse his readers. Moreover, the sexual partners of Patty are often portrayed as gay or bisexual, and in the film *Laberinto de pasiones* she herself is played by a drag queen named Fabio/Fanny McNamara. The Patty Diphusa narrative thus undercuts mass-produced heterosexual pornography by imbuing it with a queer perspective that not only parodies straight sexuality but, as Earl Jackson Jr. demonstrates in his analysis of gay male pornography, destabilizes heterosexual masculinity and femininity by reworking the dialectic of the objectifying male gaze and its object of desire.

Patty Diphusa identifies herself as a porn star in the process of writing her memoirs. In the "real" life she narrates, as in the pornography she performs, her sexuality is continually objectified. Through her autobiographical persona, however, her "reality" becomes a re-representation that she not only passively embodies but also actively interprets. With a self-assuredness typical of traditional, bourgeois life writers, she explains her decision to become an autobiographer in the following terms:

> Quiero decir que me convencí inmediatamente de que lo mejor y más interesante era YO MISMA. Y me encantó que se me ocurriera, porque lo considero un tema no sólo actual sino también bastante original, pues hasta ahora a nadie se le había ocurrido hablar sobre MI. (17)

> [What I mean is that I was immediately convinced that the best and most interesting thing to write about was MYSELF. And I love that I thought of it, because it's not only a current topic [Patty's sex life, Almodóvar's film career, or queer sexuality in general], but it's also pretty original, since up until now nobody's thought of writing about ME. (5)]

From the outset, Patty recognizes the difficulties inherent in autobiographical prosopopeia and how "cuando una escribe muchas veces te salen cosas ligeramente falsas" (21) ["when you write, often slightly false things will come out" (9)]. This is due not only to the fact that the self appears solely through the drag of language (despite whatever lingering illusions an even up-to-date autobiographer like Patty might hold regarding the possibility of an extradiscursive self), but to the more immediate problem that the drag donned by self-writers is never entirely of their own creation but is a social product, though as Patty adds, critics often do call the slightly false things of autobiography a creation (21). The drag of the autobiographical text is hence not a mask, since a mask implies the existence of something concealed (and Patty after all has nothing to hide), but a kind of undercurrent through which the assertion of selfhood is incessantly "dragged" back and objectified in terms of dominant patterns of identity. This oscillation between an elusive freedom and its forever imminent and ineluctable reification (the fundamental tension of both the praxis of camp and the autobiographical gesture itself), achieves a critical moment in the text of Almodóvar through the representation of rape.

In the second chapter of her memoirs, Patty recounts being sexually assaulted.[4] On one level the narrative simply reproduces heterosexual violence and can in fact be read as Almodóvar's own fantasy of either raping or being raped. He nevertheless queers the scene by reading it through Patty's camp perspective (and to a lesser degree through a bisexual assailant who would rather watch from the sidelines). Patty seemingly ignores the violence to which she is subjected and remains focused on the surface plane of her body, responding not to the violation of her being but her appearance: "Que a una la violen dos sicópatas es normal, pero que después me dejaran tirada en la Casa de Campo, de madrugada y con una pinta como de película mejicana de vampiros, no lo soporto" (25) ["Getting raped by two psychopaths is normal, but when they leave you stranded at the Casa de Campo very late at night looking like you stepped out of a Mexican vampire movie, that I can't stand" (12)]. By inverting the normal/abnormal binary, and more precisely by flattening her identity to that of a screen image from a low-budget, "low-culture" film, which is itself a kitsch rendition of an established genre, Patty aims to minimize the violence done to her. In so doing she does not react to her oppressors but instead reimagines herself and her surroundings: "El Asesino me volvió a dar una hostia para que me callara, entonces yo me dediqué a hacer un ejercicio de relajación: pensé que estaba en una isla desierta, tomando el sol desnuda, arrullada por el murmullo del mar y acariciada por la brisa del Caribe" (24) ["The Murderer smacked me again to shut me up, at which point I started to do a relaxation exercise: I imagined I was on a desert island, lying nude in the sun, lulled by the murmur of the sea and caressed by the Caribbean breeze" (12)]. As a consequence of her fantasy, she eventually becomes oblivious to the rape itself, troubled solely by the difficulty of finding a taxi at a late hour in Madrid, since "todo el mundo conoce los problemas de transporte que hay en Madrid" (25) ["everyone knows how hard it is to get around in Madrid" (12)].

As these passages reveal, the focus of Almodóvar is ultimately not rape itself but the means through which the reality of rape is silenced — either in imitation of the discourse of misogyny, as his detractors would undoubtedly have it, or in a concerted effort to anesthetize its effects through an act of imagination. Because of her ordeal, Patty decides "que hay situaciones en que a las mujeres no les queda más remedio que hacerse feministas" (25) ["that there are situations in which women have no choice but to become feminists" (12)]. Yet despite her intentions, her "feminism" lacks practical efficacy. She herself manages to disregard the violence perpetrated against her, but violence remains, as the autobiography of Reinaldo Arenas makes all too clear, even in the idyllic Caribbean world of her fancies.[5] Patty reappropriates hegemonic norms in an effort to introduce a wedge between oppressor and oppressed. But as Leo Bersani writes in his discussion of Judith Butler's *Bodies That Matter,* such a move "partly subverts [these norms] *and* partly reidealizes them" (51; emphasis added). This, then, is the contradiction of camp informing Almodóvar's entire written and filmic production.

Who's Looking Now?

The dynamics of Almodovarian camp are made explicit through a shifting and contestatory gaze that ultimately eludes the grasp of even the ingenious Patty. In one sense she succeeds in subverting the heterosexual male gaze, not only by subjecting it to her own ostensibly female gaze, but also by forcing it back upon itself. In a chapter titled "El lenguaje es una convención o el novio amnésico de Ana Conda" ["Language Is a Convention; or, Ana Conda's Amnesiac Boyfriend"], Patty receives a phone call from a man who has supposedly lost his memory. She is intrigued by his voice and asks him to describe his body, which he cannot remember, by looking at his reflection in the glass of the phone booth. As Patty guides his reading of his body, she becomes sexually aroused,[6] while he is progressively hypnotized by his own self-image.

> — Háblame de tu cuerpo. ¿Cómo eres?
> — Pues no lo sé.
> — Mírate en los cristales de la cabina y descríbete.
> — Parezco joven. Veinte o veintidós años.
>   Empezó a describirse lentamente como quien está LEYENDO. O era cierto todo aquel montaje o era el mejor locutor del mundo.
> — ¿Guapo?
> — Sí.
> — ¿Altura?
> — Un metro ochenta, tal vez más. Soy delgado, pero correcto según el modelo griego. Llevo pantalón vaquero.
> — Métete la mano en la bragueta y describe lo que encuentres.

— Ya puedes imaginártelo.

— A Estas Horas mi IMAGINACION se confunde con mis DESEOS, y mis deseos no tienen MEDIDA. Sé MAS CONCRETO.

— La naturaleza ha sido muy generosa conmigo.

— Odio los eufemismos, pero me fiaré de ti. ¿Ojos?

— Claros. Verdes o azules.

— ¿Iluminan de un modo extraordinario tu mirada? ¿Te hipnotizan cuando miras en el cristal, sin poder apartar la mirada de ellos?

— Pues sí, es exactamente como tú dices. (44–45)

[— Tell me about your body. What's it like.

— Uh, I don't know.

— Look at your reflection in the phone booth windows and tell me what you see.

— I'm young. Twenty or twenty-two.

He started describing himself slowly as if he were READING. Either everything he said was true or he was the best speaker in the world.

— Good looking?

— Yeah.

— Height?

— Six-one, maybe taller. I'm thin, but well proportioned, according to the Greek model. I'm wearing jeans.

— Stick your hand in your crotch and tell me what you find.

— You can imagine.

— At This Time of Day my IMAGINATION gets confused with my DESIRES, and my desires don't have a SIZE. Be MORE CONCRETE.

— Nature has been very generous.

— I hate euphemisms, but I'll trust you. Eyes?

— Blue or green.

— Do they light up your face in some extraordinary way? Do they hypnotize you as you look into the glass so that you find it hard to turn your eyes away?

— Well yeah, it's exactly as you say. (30–31)]

The caller's self-reflection and subsequent self-enchantment in the phone booth (a site of communication transformed through anonymous phone sex into the locus of an act of narcissism) undercuts his apparent heterosexual masculinity. The agent of the maneuver is Patty, whose overarching female gaze objectifies the male body. The male body, however, does not become the converse of the "blinded" female body of dominant masculine heterosexual discourse since its gaze is ultimately not deactivated but instead refracted from its binary opposite to itself. Through the directed reading of Patty, the caller is thus constituted as an object of a female as well as a male gaze. This latter gaze in fact elicits a gay male subject position to the extent that it identifies with the male body while simultaneously positing the male body as an object of desire.

The phone-booth passage is analogous to the quasi-(gay)pornographic scene at the beginning of *La ley del deseo.* According to Jackson, this shot functions to interrupt the heterosexual Oedipal narrative (131) by conflating what in Freud are the mutually exclusive terms of identification and desire (139). Like the implicit viewer of the film, the caller in *Patty Diphusa* is induced to posit the male body as an object of both identification and desire. As a consequence, he opposes the "law of the father" and, in keeping with Jackson's rereading of Mulvey, assumes the dual role of "bearer of the look." (Through the egological split of his narcissistic gesture he concomitantly "wields" and "sustains" the desiring male gaze [cf. Jackson 143; Mulvey 18].) For this reason he stands as a locus of sexual difference within and in contradistinction to the ostensibly heterosexual narrative of the Patty Diphusa text.

Although all of Patty's sexual partners appear to be male, in some instances their gender is clearly only an appearance. On one occasion Patty meets a person named Juan Félix in a cafe over breakfast. After eating, she goes to the bathroom. When she looks up, she discovers Juan Félix standing in the doorway of the stall watching her. Because he is wearing dark Raybans, he apparently sees little. Patty, on the other hand, manages to scrutinize his reflection in the mirror while she fixes her lipstick. She asks him if his Raybans are real, which he confirms, and then informs him that hers are fake, suggesting that while his scope of vision is darkened, hers is unimpeded by the blinders traditionally imposed on the female gaze. Yet in this instance her artificial lens on the world prevents her from seeing her way clear, and after returning home and having sex, she learns that her partner was once a woman, and an old school friend at that, who loved her for years and underwent a sex-change operation precisely in order to attract her. For Patty, however, Juan Félix is still essentially "Adela," and her rejection of the latter might be taken as a sign that she is actually a heterosexual woman — though it could just as easily be interpreted as the action of a gay man in drag. (As Patty herself has admitted, she is never certain which rest room to use. And if that were not enough, she meets the only man she really likes while riding in his cab and listening to the song "It's Raining Men" by the Weather Girls, perhaps the most famous icons of the gay disco scene of the early eighties.)

The sexual identity of Patty is even more thoroughly problematized through a highly unusual reconfiguration of the Oedipal motif. In a chapter titled "Un episodio burgués" ["A Bourgeois Episode"], Patty takes a young lover, Pepón, whom she hires as a secretary to help type her memoirs. The scenario that follows is reworked in *La ley del deseo*. In *Patty Diphusa*, Patty is supposedly generating the text as she protagonizes it. In *La ley del deseo*, the lead character, Pablo, is writing the script of the film as he performs in it.[7] One of his lovers, Antonio, is the child of an overly possessive and homophobic mother who attempts to thwart her son's sexual relationships by enforcing the heterosexual law of an absent father.[8] The mother of Pepón, in contrast, undercuts heterosexual normativity through her explicit desire for him. According to this inscription of the Oedipal narrative, the mother regards Patty as a rival, and in an effort to blunt her competitive edge, ascribes to her the identity of transvestite, transforming her, albeit fleetingly, from a woman into a man, and given Patty's relationship with Pepón, into what is for all intents and purposes a gay man. In a moment of extreme gender and sexual ambiguity, Patty is subjected to the queer gaze of a hypermasculinized (and, as such, in drag) mother/son couple: "madre e hijo me miraron como cuando Superman echa rayos por los ojos" (81) ["mother and son were looking at me like Superman with his X-ray vision" (63)]. As a consequence she is overcome by a sort of reverse castration anxiety (if she is not careful, after all, she might actually be endowed with a phallus). Only later does she learn that Pepón deceived his mother in order to prevent her from destroying their relationship:

Mi madre está muy mal, desde que murió mi padre hace ocho años se ha obsesionado conmigo porque soy igual que él. Está enamorada de mí. No le importa que me acueste con chicos, dice que «eso es distinto, porque no pueden competir con ella», pero no soporta que lo haga con chicas. Pretende ser la única mujer de mi vida, por eso cuando me voy con chicas que es lo que realmente me gusta tengo que engañarla. Por eso le dije que eras un travestí. (83)

[My mother isn't well. Since my father died eight years ago she's been obsessed with me because I look just like him. She's in love with me. She doesn't

care if I sleep with guys. She says "that's different" because they're not competing with her. But she can't stand that I do it with girls. She wants to be the
only woman in my life, so when I go with girls, which is what I really like, I've
got to fool her. That's why I told her you were a transvestite. (64)]

This episode is significant in that it functions to invert the homosexual/
heterosexual binary. Here the dominant gaze, wielded by the incestuous Oedipal couple, contrives to constitute a "normal" homosexuality in spite of
Pepón's subsequent confession and the fact that "that's different." In the process heterosexuality is closeted. Indeed, its truth can be uttered only in secret
and in opposition to the "law of the mother." Patty, of course, respects no
law and equates the suppression of her womanhood with a class oppression
requiring nothing short of revolutionary action: " — Señora, comprendo
que haya países en los que los campesinos les corten las cabezas a sus señoras"
(82–83) [" — Ma'am, understand that in some countries the peasants cut
their mistresses' heads off" (64)]. The menacing words of Patty are nonetheless a parody of real resistance: "En ocasiones me sale una conciencia social
tremenda. No soportaba estar ni un minuto más en aquella casa. Recogí mi
bolso, me tiré un pedo y me fui" (83) ["Sometimes my tremendous social
conscience comes out. I couldn't stand being in that house another minute.
I grabbed my bag, farted and left" (64)]. Patty cleverly employs camp in order to deactivate the camp gaze of the mother and establish her own identity
as a "real" and "natural" woman. But for the time being, at least, the artificial
renders only the artificial, and the identity of Patty remains ungrounded.

As autobiographer Patty in fact declares that she initiated her "life" not
with the intention of asserting a discrete identity, as do such "serious" gay
life writers as Roig, Goytisolo, and Gil de Biedma, but with the more modest
aspiration of proving that she possessed a typewriter. By her very admission,
therefore, she has nothing to express other than the instrument of expression
itself — be it the typewriter or her own peculiar camp posturing. Despite
her persistent claims to womanhood, her only "inherent" value is "la alegría,
la desvergüenza, la frivolidad y el ingenio" (87) ["happiness, shamelessness,
frivolousness and ingenuity" (69)], that is, her lack of a fixed essence. This
freedom from essence, however, is not affirmed as a model for others, and
she blatantly rejects "toda la pandilla de ineptos lectores" (87–88) ["the
whole inept gang of readers" (69)] who dares to read her and to identify with

her. In an ironic twist, then, nonessence constitutes her uniqueness, while simultaneously setting her apart, and above, her social milieu.

Writing nevertheless drags her back down again. Although she might deem her memoirs to be the most significant piece of Spanish-language writing in recent centuries, surpassing in fame even *Cien años de soledad* [One hundred years of solitude], the popularity of her work ultimately functions to reestablish the supremacy of the other in her life, and she admits that if she had realized beforehand the consequences, she would never have written a single line. In a decidedly "uncamplike" moment, she seeks refuge in a spirit of seriousness, claiming (albeit unconvincingly) to prefer such solid "virtues" as country music, the family, Soviet communism, common sense, and roots (90). The success of her undertaking thus seems to have silenced her just as effectively as failure silenced Roig, leading her to conclude that she has nothing more to say: "Esta página, a partir de este momento, estará vacía. Que la rellenen otros" (90) ["This page, after this sentence will be empty. Let the others fill it up" (72)]. Her words, of course, should not be taken at face value, for whereas the rest of the page is left blank, she proceeds to speak a little while longer.

Autobiographical Voyeurism

The last chapter of the Patty Diphusa narrative in fact reveals a struggle over the final word. In a dialogue between Patty and Pedro, titled "Yo, Patty, intento conocerme a mí misma a través de mi autor" (91) ["I, Patty, Try to Get to Know Myself through My Author"], she announces her intention to expose him: "Hacía tiempo que quería desnudar a mi autor" (91) ["I've been wanting to expose my author for some time now" (73)]. In this context not only is identity hetero-relational but self-knowledge requires that the other actually be "outed." Once Pedro is made visible, Patty comes straight to the point: "En primer lugar, me gustaría saber si soy hombre, mujer o travestón" (91) ["In the first place, I'd like to know if I'm a man, woman or transvestite" (73)]. The response, "Eres una mujer, naturalmente" (91) ["You're a woman, naturally" (73)], might seem to settle the issue once and for all. Yet to the extent that the self is mediated by the other, identity continues to escape her. Pedro ostensibly holds the key to her being, but when she asks if she is no more than his alter ego, he informs her that ultimately she is the product of the reader's fantasy. He, therefore, is her creator only insofar as he too reads her:

> PATTY. — ¿Tú lees mis memorias?
> PEDRO. — Las leo una vez para ver cuántos errores de impresión hay, y desesperarme después.
> PATTY. — O sea, que también eres un lector. O sea, que a ti también te gustaría ser como yo. (92)
>
> [PATTY — Did you read my memoirs?
> PEDRO — I read them once through to see how many printer's errors there are and got very upset.
> PATTY — So you're a reader too. That is, you also want to be like me. (74)]

Since Pedro reads Patty (even though he might do so only in order to imitate her) he is clearly the subject and she the object of a reifying gaze. In an effort to reappropriate and redirect this gaze, Patty resumes her initial project of exposure, approaching Pedro for a sexual intimacy that he subsequently declines:

> PATTY. — Háblame más de mí, mientras te hago alguna cosita.
> PEDRO. — No quiero que me hagas nada. (93)
>
> [PATTY — Tell me a little more about myself while I do something to you.
> PEDRO — I don't want you to do anything to me. (75)]

Pedro persists in holding her hostage to his gaze by reading her advances as part of his own onanistic fantasy: "Estáte quieta. Si quiero masturbarme sé muy bien cómo hacerlo" (93) ["Relax. If I want to masturbate I know very well how to do it" (75)]. But Patty remains focused on his physical characteristics, and specifically his stocky legs, which he claims to have inherited from Oscar Wilde. Through identification with Wilde, Pedro deessentializes his own ostensibly masculine persona, and in so doing thwarts the effort of Patty to use him as a means for grounding her femininity. He nevertheless continues to assert an all-knowing eye that in the end succeeds in reducing Patty to silent objectivity:

PATTY. — Pedro, creo que después de esta entrevista sigo sin saber nada de ti.
PEDRO. — Sin embargo yo de ti lo sabía ya todo. (95)

[PATTY — Pedro, the interview's over and I still don't know anything about you.
PEDRO — Yeah, but I already knew everything about you. (77)][9]

On one level this passage reaffirms the epistemic structures of patriarchy: the male wields and the female sustains the reifying gaze. As a consequence not only is the woman "blinded" but the gay male specter haunting the entire text is exorcised from the picture.

By staging the scenario in this way Almodóvar seemingly reverses the "descriptive" thrust of traditional autobiography: it is not the inscribed self that eludes him (as occurs with gay life writers) but he who eludes self-inscription. Through the Patty Diphusa narrative Almodóvar actually disavows the entire autobiographical genre, choosing instead, like Villena, to "unwrite" his life by projecting a patently fictional persona (Patty) from whom he withdraws. Yet the self that withdraws (Pedro) is itself also textual, incapable either of affirming or negating the ontological integrity of the author. What is more, though Almodóvar eschews a narcissistic fusion (whether conceived of as ontological or erotic) of the writing and written selves, he remains enchanted by the allure of the self, casting a narcissistic gaze that ultimately functions as a kind of "autobiographical voyeurism": "Pues yo me miro en el espejo y me excito" (94) ["Hey, I get turned on looking at myself in the mirror" (76)]. As in the phone-booth scene, this gaze reestablishes a gay male subject position. To the extent that it is effected through the mediation of Patty, her project of "outing" is completed, and Almodóvar, willy-nilly, appears as gay.

The basic reflexive gesture of Almodóvar's final gaze in fact subsumes the multiple reflections of his written (and filmic)[10] texts: Patty reflecting on a self and a world that are themselves the reflection of a text (reality imitates porno); Patty and Pedro mirroring (and struggling to possess) one another; and Almodóvar fantasizing the sex life of Patty, the relationship of Patty and Pedro, and Patty/Pedro as both his objective image and the bifurcated object of his own self-desire. But as indicated in the "Autoentrevista" ["Self-Interview"] that follows the Patty Diphusa narrative, Almodovarian desire remains unfulfilled. This is due less to the inexorable condition of an existential subject, forever desiring the being that it lacks but that it can never achieve, than to the fact that for Almodóvar desire is itself the object of a law that constitutes it in perpetual alterity. This law is precisely language, and more specifically writing, in that a law, etymologically speaking, involves an act of "laying down" or "fixing." In keeping with the notion of homographesis, the laying down (on paper) and the fixing (in words) of desire simultaneously inscribes and describes desire, and for the Almodovarian personae writing is hence an experience of both consolation and despair. In a piece titled "Un buen comienzo" ["A Good Start"], which echoes various passages from the Patty Diphusa narrative, a fictional writer explains:

> Yo sólo escribo los domingos. No importa a la hora que me despierte ni con quién, todos los domingos me levanto con ganas de llorar. Entonces lloro y escribo. Después siento una agradable melancolía. Pero no sé por qué le cuento todo esto. (130)

> [I only write on Sundays. It doesn't matter what time I get up or with whom, every Sunday I get up wanting to cry. So I cry and I write. After that I feel a comfortable melancholy. But I don't know why I'm telling you all this. (111)]

To which his interlocutor, a woman much like Patty, simply responds: " — Yo tampoco" (130) ["Me neither" (111)]. In spite of the ontological "impossibility" of the autobiographical project, Almodóvar, like all autobiographers according to the Rousseauian dictum and gay and queer life writers in particular, thus reveals an overpowering need to tell, and through telling, to assert himself against the discourses of the world.

PART THREE

Homobiography

CHAPTER SEVEN

Juan Goytisolo with Birds of a Feather

Though Almodóvar challenges the ideology of identity through his queering of gender and sexuality, the narrative gaze at the end of the Patty Diphusa text turns inward in a reflective gesture that functions to isolate the autobiographical subject on a reef of solipsism. In *Las virtudes del pájaro solitario* [*The Virtues of the Solitary Bird*], in contrast, reflection is not a solitary enterprise of the queer (the "pájaro," or "bird," of the Cuban slang that Goytisolo appropriates) but a reciprocal act through which the self and its companions recognize a mutual sameness. This sameness is initially communicated through the discursive structures of AIDS — a "communicable" and ultimately fatal deficiency that reverses the "life" sign, thereby rendering the sign of "death," or "thanatos." As an instance of AIDS writing, *Las virtudes del pájaro solitario* inscribes "thanatos" as the overdetermining signifier of homoeroticism: "soy de una gente que cuando aman, mueren" (152) ["I come from a people who, when they love, die" (140)].[1] But this inscription, through the process of homographesis, is simultaneously a de-scription that Goytisolo presses into a "bios," not as a hetero-ized "life" but as a common course or way undertaken by homos (and in particular the homo-writer and homo-reader) at this most critical moment of their history. Whereas in gay autobiography the self is forever slipping into the alterity of hetero-relationality, in queer life writing the self/other binary is subverted while reducing the self to a narcissistic gaze. In homobiography the self and the other are united through similitude. As represented in *Las virtudes del pájaro solitario* each is at once a singularity (a solitary bird) and a plurality (the flock) that, although confined within the overarching cage of hetero-relationality, stands poised in the end to take flight in pursuit of a common end.

AIDS Writing

At the outset of his autobiographical venture Goytisolo reveals an intention to inform his readers of "quien pudiste ser y no has sido" (*Coto vedado* 29) ["whom you might have been and have not become" (*Forbidden Territory* 21)]; yet at the conclusion of *En los reinos de taifa* he admits an inability to grasp an autonomous and authentic self. The self of the autobiographical volumes remains caught in a web of hetero-relationality that permits its expression solely in opposition to its other — be it the heterosexual, masculine, Spanish, Castilian, Catholic, or fascistic other of Goytisolo's early years. What is more, despite his compassion for certain individual lesbians and gay men (the girls in the Cuban youth camp, his grandfather Ricardo, Virgilio Piñera, and so forth), throughout most of the period recounted in the autobiographies Goytisolo experiences little solidarity with a larger gay and lesbian community. Prior to his coming out he thus writes:

> Mi actitud condescendiente y burlona es la de un español estreñido como los militantes políticos con quienes me trato. Las bromas y opiniones reprobadoras sobre las *locas* que oigo diariamente a mi alrededor, las adopto por propias: me asomo a las sordideces y miserias del gueto, pero pertenezco a la urbe exterior, limpia y planificada. (*En los reinos de taifa* 215)

> [My condescending, mocking attitude was that of an uptight Spaniard, like the political militants I went about with. I adopted as my own the jokes and reproving opinions toward the queens that I heard daily around me: I dropped in on the sordid misery of the ghetto, but I belonged to the planned clean city outside. (*Realms of Strife* 182)]

In *Las virtudes del pájaro solitario,* which was published two years after his autobiography, any such masculinist bias has disappeared. The catalyst for the change in his conception of gay sexuality and the structuration of the self and the other is AIDS. Although *Las virtudes del pájaro solitario,* like so much of Goytisolo's fiction, contains numerous examples of autobiographical prosopopeia, it in fact has more in common with what has come to be known as AIDS writing.

AIDS writing is characterized by a tremendous urgency on the part of writers not only to respond to an immediate crisis but often merely to complete the writing project before dying. Michael Denneny seeks antecedents for AIDS writing in the trench poetry of World War I and the testimonies of the Holocaust but, as he points out, most of these texts were published and read at a later date (46). Even Anne Frank, who documented her day-to-day life during the Holocaust, did so without actually knowing her ultimate fate at the hands of the Nazis (Denneny 47). AIDS writers, on the other hand, are in the midst of a battle and are also acutely aware from the start of the outcome of their struggle. Goytisolo, nonetheless, does not write as a PWA (person with AIDS), and rather than a personal testimony, *Las virtudes del pájaro solitario* stands as what Linda Gould Levine, in contrast to Susan Sontag's negative reading of AIDS in *AIDS and Its Metaphors,* has called a "compensatory myth" of the disease through which "la figura del virus-plaga-castigo-metáfora malévola del siglo XX deja de ser 'homo-sida'" ("El papel" 235) [the figure of the malevolent virus-plague-punishment-metaphor of the twentieth century ceases to be "homo-AIDS/homo-cidal" (trans. mine)].[2]

AIDS writing directly engages PWAs as well as, though by no means exclusively, gay men in general. The notion of AIDS as an inherently gay illness has been medically debunked, but as Les Wright argues, "as a collectively experienced catastrophe, AIDS *has been* a gay disease" (68). This is because AIDS, in spite of its incidence among women and heterosexuals, continues to be identified in the popular imagination with the gay male.[3] As Simon Watney remarks, epidemiology has been displaced "by a moralised etiology of disease, which regards AIDS as an intrinsic property of the fantasised 'homosexual body'" (54). According to Emmanuel S. Nelson, this displacement has resulted in a "radical (re)othering and (re)medicalizing" (2) of the gay male. The conflation of AIDS and gay male sexuality has nevertheless prompted the lesbian and gay community to reassess its received notions of sexuality and identity.

For David Van Leer, AIDS writing, and in particular the academic discourse of AIDS, tends to privilege the disease over other illnesses and in so doing runs the risk of creating a hierarchy of those most deserving to live. "Gay male rhetoric," he aptly warns, "must guard against formulations that, in complaining that 'we' are not supposed to die this way, implicitly posit the existence of a number of 'theys' (the aged, the economically underprivileged, other races or nations) whose comparable deaths are more in line with the nature of things" (152–53). Van Leer further maintains that AIDS discourse is predicated on the supposition that AIDS has been mis-represented in the dominant media and that through a process of resignification, it might be more effectively combated. He argues, however, that the disease is not equivalent to a knowledge of the disease and reminds us that in the end "people die of opportunistic infections, not mis-representation" (144). Yet mis-representation can indeed produce conditions that hasten death, whether through the neglect of agencies responsible for developing therapies and providing health care or through an internalized homophobia that discourages PWAs from seeking early treatment and blinds others to the possibility that they might actually be susceptible to infection. (Various commentators, for example, describe a tendency among certain Latino males to engage in same-sex activity while identifying themselves as straight, and hence as immune to what they perceive to be an intrinsically gay and white disease [Alonso and Koreck 122].) Re-representation is therefore a real instrument of survival. Though it might not lead to a cure, it will still, as Van Leer remarks, "keep visible an issue which even in the liberal academy is already beginning to seem someone else's problem, or yesterday's news" (156).

In reflecting on the representation of AIDS, Van Leer seeks to demonstrate what, on the basis of Sartrean ontology, might be called the "transphenomenality" of the disease, and ultimately to affirm the existence of a being that forms the condition of all representation: "The very notion of representation entails a distinction between being and seeming — between how things are in the world and how they are construed. This distinction between being and seeming in turn requires at least the logical possibility of being — of the existence of unconstructed things, which may or may not be knowable. . . . Thus even as they reduce AIDS to its representations, social constructionists implicitly reaffirm the existence of a reality not reducible to those representations" (143). Van Leer's discussion in fact echoes the Sartrean tenet that being is the prerequisite of all appearance of being, although for Sartre this is a purely "logical" condition since being can be perceived

only to the extent that it appears. For Sartre, furthermore, disease is not a being but a meaning or unity that consciousness ascribes to such contingent
phenomena as pain (*Being and Nothingness* 443). In most cases, of course,
AIDS is first posited not by PWAs, as the synthetic unity of discrete physical
conditions or pains they may or may not have yet experienced, but through
the pronouncement of the other (most often in oral consultation) who reads
their bodies as sero-positive. In the prevailing medical (as well as popular)
discourse of AIDS, the utterance of sero-positivity is analogous to a death
sentence. The internalization of such a sentence marks what Sartre describes
as the "triumph of the point of view of the Other over the point of view
which I am toward myself" (691). But from the internal perspective of consciousness, its death remains a contradiction — a fiction that ultimately can
be "known" only by the other (or by consciousness inasmuch as it attempts
to assume the vantage point of the other), and then only in exteriority. This
is because consciousness, on the level of pure reflection elucidated by Sartre,
is conscious of itself solely as a *project* of being, and death is the very annihilation of all possible projects of consciousness. "My project toward a particular death is comprehensible (suicide, martyrdom, heroism) but not the
project toward *my* death as the undetermined possibility of no longer realizing a presence in the world, for this project would be the destruction of all
projects. Thus death can not be my peculiar possibility; it can not even be
one of *my* possibilities" (691). Whereas death is a logical certainty, an existential intuition of "my" death is hence, according to the Sartrean scheme,
impossible. In *Las virtudes del pájaro solitario* Goytisolo capitalizes on this
existential conundrum, re-representing AIDS not as the annihilation of the
self but as a means of affirming life and of achieving homo-reciprocity.

Wind in a Net

In *Las virtudes del pájaro solitario* Goytisolo aims to recreate an ancient text
that has either been lost or made to disappear: the legendary *Tratado de las
propiedades del pájaro solitario* [Treatise on the properties of the solitary bird]
of San Juan de la Cruz.[4] It is his implicit contention that the entire poetic
corpus of San Juan de la Cruz is imbued not only with an "unorthodox" Islamic and Jewish mystical discourse, as is commonly maintained, but also

with a decidedly homoerotic dimension, and he thus undertakes *Las virtudes del pájaro solitario* as a reinscription of a silenced gay voice.[5] Notwithstanding this, the question regarding the sexuality of San Juan de la Cruz is unanswerable. In his poetry he represents himself as a woman, but in so doing he merely reiterates the centuries-old conventions of mystical discourse wherein the soul is depicted as the feminine counterpart in a love relationship with a masculine God. Moreover, despite whatever homoerotic fantasies or actual sex San Juan de la Cruz might have experienced, he could not have been gay in the modern sense of the term precisely because the conditions necessary for the construction of a homosexual identity did not fully exist in sixteenth-century Spain. Yet for Goytisolo his poetic texts can be read, and rewritten, in a way that challenges the rhetorical structures of hetero-relationality and energizes gay men and PWAs within various contemporary social and cultural contexts.[6] The writing of San Juan de la Cruz is in fact relevant to the articulation of homo-relationality, not only because it envisions a union with the other (as opposed to an assertion of the self in contradistinction to the other) but also insofar as it expresses, in the turning point of the dark night when the self-effacing mystic is emptied even of the desire for God, an indifference to difference. This indifference to difference undoes the self as posited within hetero-relationality and leads to an increasing, albeit never fully realized, similitude of self and other.

The narrator of *Las virtudes del pájaro solitario* appears, among his many guises, as a scholar of Sanjuanist mysticism speculating on the possibility of locating within the writing of San Juan de la Cruz a fixed and decipherable meaning: "era posible . . . hallar una clave explicativa unívoca, . . . establecer una rigurosa crítica filológica, buscar una significación estrictamente literal, . . . capturar la sutileza del viento con una red?" (59) ["was it possible to . . . find a univocal explanatory key, . . . establish a rigorous philological critique, search out a strictly literal meaning, . . . capture the subtlety of wind in a net?" (55)]. He realizes, however, that though this is the goal of the rational method of textual analysis, rationality is incapable of accomplishing it to the extent that the unitary meanings it imposes on the text, while on one level repeating the text itself, invariably slip into hetero-relationality. Its glosses, "en vez de aclarar su sentido . . . lo envuelven en una compleja red hermenéutica redundante y contradictoria" (151) ["instead of shedding light on its sense . . . envelop it in a complex hermeneutical net at once redundant and contradictory" (139)]. Rather than reinforce this discursive framework through an analytical exegesis, the narrator therefore strives to free language from the shackles of rationality and "abandonarlo al campo magnético de sus imantaciones secretas" (59) ["abandon it to the magnetic field of its secret attractions" (55)]. These secret attractions, which propel his undertaking, are not those of the same for the different but of the same for the same. In the Sanjuanist text the mechanism of "homo-attraction" is represented specifically as the divine word — the spirit or wind breathed within the soul through which the soul and God are united. In rereading and rewriting San Juan de la Cruz, the Goytisolo narrator will reconfigure the Sanjuanist image of the word, making it an instrument of destruction (the annihilating discourse of AIDS) as well as a means through which a homo-unity is ultimately achieved.

In fact the narrator of *Las virtudes del pájaro solitario* reveals a multifaceted persona whose roles include those of scholar, mystic poet, PWA, and Goytisolo himself. His trajectory in the text is not linear but circular (as if he were spinning downward through the vortex of the mystical dark night), and entire sentences and passages are repeated as his voice retraces the same psychological and social terrain, albeit from different vantage points. Among the numerous scenes are a gay bathhouse in Paris, the jail cell in the Toledo monastery in which San Juan de la Cruz was imprisoned, an aviary, and a sports stadium. The latter is reminiscent of the site of the communist youth rally described in *Coto vedado* as well as the Havana stadium where, according to the documentary film *Conducta Impropia* [Improper conduct] of Néstor Almendros and Orlando Jiménez-Leal, Cuban gays of the 1960s were confined before being transferred to the forced-labor camps: the Unidades Militares de Ayuda a la Producción, or UMAP [Military units for production assistance].[7] An even more significant setting than the stadium is the sanitarium wherein the AIDS-afflicted narrator has been interned. Situated on a tropical island, it evokes the forced quarantine sites of many Cuban AIDS patients.[8]

AIDS is represented in *Las virtudes del pájaro solitario* like a vision from an apocalyptic nightmare: it is an old and haggard woman with a witch's finger and the wings of a vampire, whose arrival on "an unlucky date" was foreseen in secret astrological treatises on the plagues of the end of the millennium, and whose intrusion "desbarataba de rondón nuestras vidas" (12) ["abruptly ruined our lives" (14)]. It is a blood curse, distinguishing the Semite from the Christian, the mystic reformer from the Inquisitor, and above all the gays from the straights. AIDS is first perceived by a collective subject: "había aparecido, se *nos* había aparecido" (9; emphasis added) ["the apparition had materialized, had appeared to *us*" (11; emphasis added)]. This collective gay subject is immediately fragmented, and in the following sentence the narrator's use of a second-person plural indicates the beginning of his separation from his companions. Through the advent of AIDS, the reciprocal "nos/us" will be splintered into a "yo/I" and "vosotros/you" and elsewhere an "él/he," "ella/she," and so forth. This is the major temporal occurrence of the text and, from the perspective of the narrative voice, the pivotal event in all of human history. With the eruption of AIDS in the world, the world was "para siempre dividido en dos, antes y después de la condenación" (19) ["forever divided in two, before and after the condemnation" (20)]. The temporal dislocation wrought by AIDS is also a logical dislocation of hetero-relationality, borne out not only on the pronominal level of the text but also through the AIDS/non-AIDS binary itself, which for Goytisolo is the radical (and "millennial") expression of the homo/hetero binary as posited at the end of the nineteenth century.

As a result of AIDS, the narrator and his companions are violently thrust from the ghettoized world that they heretofore inhabited. While they imagined this world as a zone of safety, it was not immune to external forces, nor was it ever even more than an imitation of the outside sphere from which its occupants sought refuge. As in a theater, everything was faked, from the mise en scène to the recited lines to the mimed gestures. "Life" within was a performance, and in the immediate wake of AIDS the narrator clings to his drag as the only identity he has known. (He thus differs from the Lorquian Director who would fashion an authentic mask to correspond to his repressed, inner self.) Once outside, however, this drag makes him easy prey for his assailants: "todo contribuía a obstaculizar la desigual carrera, el talón agudo de mis zapatos se torcía" (27) ["everything contributed to making the race an unequal one, putting obstacles in my path, the stiletto heels of my pumps got twisted" (27)]. Drag in this case is unable to subvert dominant configurations of identity and instead "trips up" the queer, who is finally caught like a bird in a net and reinterned, not in the darkened world of the closet, but in a well-lighted clinic where all watch and await his eventual demise.

At the end of the first scene the narrator asks why those affected, either directly or indirectly, by AIDS have failed to take action. His response is that they have been indoctrinated into accepting their status in society as if it were an inexorable destiny. Moreover, what he calls "el brillo ofuscador de la gran máquina informativa nos había predispuesto insidiosamente a la conformidad y desánimo" (16) ["the dazzling brightness of the great information machine had insidiously predisposed us to conformity and demoralization" (18)]. This information machine (television, the media, or hetero-relational discourse in general), functions as the instrument of their alienation, reappearing in the sanitarium as a system of loudspeakers whose incessant drone silences their tentative attempts to communicate. The narrator wonders if they might rebel and defy the power of the threatening loudspeakers, but like a disenchanted Larry Kramer, he comes to the conclusion that he and those like him have interiorized the disgust and contempt of others in an endless cycle through which they incarnate the hatred of what they are seen to incarnate: "su odio inalterable a cuanto encarnábamos" (23) ["their immutable hatred for everything we embodied" (24)].

When the setting shifts to the AIDS sanitarium, a PWA appears within a hermetically sealed glass bubble designed to prevent the spread of disease while allowing for a close scrutiny and reading of his body. The reaction of the other patients to his plight is one of morbid delight. They take great pleasure in seeing one of their own suffer, hence not only blindly accepting but becoming the agents of the societal reprobation that will be their own undoing:

la muy maldita se aferraba a la vida como una lapa y nosotras le pedíamos a la enfermera que la prolongara para disfrutar del espectáculo, nos acercábamos a verla con nuestras mascarillas medio muertas de risa, cada vez más viscosa y deshidratada. . . . La viperina recibía el castigo que merecía. (34–35)

[the bloody bitch clung to life like a leech and we asked the nurse to prolong it so as to enjoy the spectacle, wearing our little masks and half dead with laughter, we went right up close to her, to get a good look at her, more viscous and dehydrated each time. . . . The viperess was getting the punishment she deserved. (33–34)]

These little masks are donned in a sinister and reverse gesture of camp that does not deflate the power of identity but reinforces the negatively consti- tuted identity of the PWA. More important, the PWA is reified precisely to the extent that he is deprived of the air with which to speak. This is also the case with his queer tormentors, whose mouths are covered through the masks. Even the uninfected are silenced, and in an ostensible effort to thwart the communication of disease, the authorities preclude queer communica- tion altogether.

As a consequence of an accident, the hapless AIDS patient is adminis- tered a hallucinatory drug. Afterward, several overlapping characters emerge, including San Juan de la Cruz and the enigmatic Ben Sida [Ben Aïds].[9] The scene, moreover, begins to fluctuate between the AIDS sanitar- ium and a scholarly conference on Muslim mysticism reminiscent of a writ- ers' seminar attended by Goytisolo in the Soviet Union and recounted at length in *En los reinos de taifa.* During this conference, it is disclosed that the accident suffered by the PWA was in reality an attack, instigated from the top of a staircase like the one in the bathhouse where the AIDS apparition was first discerned. Disease and heterosexist violence are thereby reduced to a single gesture, catapulting the narrator on a journey both within himself and across time and casting him in the role of a monk languishing in the prison cell of a Carmelite monastery in sixteenth-century Toledo.

With this change of scenario, the events leading up to the incarceration of San Juan de la Cruz are recalled. His persecutors beat on the door and break it open. He tears up and swallows his most dangerous papers but is caught with a companion and dragged off to prison. He is subsequently in- terrogated about the Semitic elements within his writing: "están conven- cidos de que existen puntos de convergencia secretos entre sus poemas y los de los visionarios y místicos de la ponzoñosa secta mahometana" (83) ["they are convinced that there exist secret points of convergence between your poems and those of the visionaries and mystics of the poisonous Moham- medan sect" (77)]. What is of most concern, however, is the homoeroticism of his vision: "evite sobre todo la relación de la noche oscura con la cámara negra de nuestros éxtasis y derretimientos" (84) ["avoid above all else telling them about the dark night with the black chamber of our ecstasies and passionate loves" (78)]. This correlation of religious and sexual dissidence is significant, for through it the discourse of AIDS, initially targeted against the gay male, is revealed as a poisonous word capable of infecting and undermining the very religious, political, and social discourses through which it was originally enunciated.

In the context of the sixteenth-century Inquisition, coupled with what Goytisolo sees as the inquisitorial practices of both Francoist Spain and Castroite Cuba, the narrator expresses a fear of death at the stake. He identifies his ancient and modern avatars explicitly as birds (in the double role of mystic and queer) and envisions them being led in a cage (*la cage aux folles?*) to an auto-da-fé in a sports stadium. As they approach death, they gradually come to rediscover their affinity as well as a new means of communication: "vínculos sutiles de connivencia más allá de las barreras lingüísticas" (50) ["subtle bonds of connivance beyond linguistic barriers" (48)]. These bonds are posited not in opposition to hetero-relationality but through an act of connivance (literally a "shutting of the eyes") and as such an indifference to difference. This connivance ultimately defuses the hetero-relational structure of AIDS discourse, leading to the realization of homo-relationality: "picoteábamos el alpiste, nos mecíamos en los columpios, agilizábamos la soltura y nitidez de los vuelos, nos comunicábamos mediante gorjeos, hallábamos al fin, *sin proponérnoslo,* el lenguaje inefable de los pájaros" (98; emphasis added) ["we pecked at the birdseed, swayed back and forth on the little swings, practiced making our flights smoother, cleaner, more agile, communicated with each other by means of trills and warbles, ending up finding, *unintentionally,* the ineffable language of the birds" (92–93; emphasis added)].[10] The singing of these queer birds is no longer a camp parody of hetero-norms but, through the conniving of Goytisolo, a reappropriation of the dehypostatized "word" of the poetic vision of San Juan de la Cruz as a homo-act and the instrument of homo-praxis.

Yet the dark night is more than the twinkling of an eye, and in keeping with Sanjuanist mysticism, the road to redemption stretches not only through fire but also downward through the spiraling waters of self-annihilation.[11] Here, the diabolical Aminadab of the Sanjuanist verses becomes the minion of the AIDS apparition, who extends her witch's finger "y dirige hacia mí secamente el cerco, las aguas, caballería de Aminadab" (132) ["and brusquely unleashes upon me the siege, the waters, the cavalry of Aminadab" (123)].[12] There is asphyxia, suction, and a swallowing-up in the sewers, as if the narrator were being flushed from the world with the dregs of creation. The images of the prison, sanitarium, and bathhouse are swept together in dizzying succession, and as he lies dying he experiences union, not with the spiritual lover of the canonical San Juan de la Cruz, but with Ben Sida, the incarnation of an infected but seminal word through which the whole ideology of illness is undone.

As the narrator awakens from his dark night, he rises like a phoenix within a magnificent aviary filled with a multitude of splendid birds of varying colors, sizes, and shapes. The very existence of this aviary, of course, with its external and internal dimensions, confirms the continuation of hetero-relationality, and the narrator rightly fears having been renetted and locked in another cage by an unseen hunter. But despite the overdeterminism of hetero-relationality, two unexpected and significant events transpire that indicate a change from the former order of things. In the first the narrator achieves, albeit fleetingly, a moment of self-identification: "entre columpios, troncos, bejucos, ramas y otros instrumentos de diversión, advertí la existencia de un diminuto espejo y me planté frente a él de una volada . . . me reconocí" (168) ["amid swings, tree trunks, lianas, branches and other play equipment, I noted the existence of a tiny mirror and in one brief flight planted myself before it . . . I recognized myself" (154)]. This self-recognition is followed, through singing, by a mutual recognition of the self and the other: "a través de gorjeos cortos y uniformes, estrofas musicales con pausas variadas, zumbidos sostenidos, cantos de líquida cadencia o una mezcla de notas dulces y broncas, nos comprendíamos e identificábamos" (168–69) ["through short and uniform warbles, musical strophes with varied pauses, sustained humming, songs of liquid cadence or a mixture of sweet and rasping notes, we understood and identified each other" (154–55)]. In this moment the entire "deviant" past, alluded to in the Semitic context as the "historia de la comunidad extinguida" (125) ["history of the destroyed community" (117)], is recovered. Homo-unity occurs precisely in the wake of the lovemaking of "I" and Ben Sida through a joint undertaking on the part of all the homo-birds: an ecstatic flight to perfection reminiscent of the night journey of Mohammed. This flight, nevertheless, will not transcend the aviary, and in completing his rescription of the legendary Sanjuanist text as well as his own homobiographical enterprise, Goytisolo writes of the solitary bird: "emprende el vuelo sin dejar de estar inmóvil, viaja sin cubrir la menor distancia, se aproxima y no recorre espacio alguno" (169) ["it begins the flight without ceasing to be immobile, travels without covering the slightest distance, draws closer and traverses no space whatsoever" (155)]. Despite this fluttering of wings, he and the other homo-birds remain stationary. Yet they manage to generate a wind, and whereas previously they stifled in "un vacío de campana neumática" (20) ["the vacuum of a bell jar" (21)], they now make viable their living space by filling it with the air with which to breathe and to utter their song.

In *Las virtudes del pájaro solitario* homo-unity is constructed, through the recognition of mutual bonds and signs of identity, across time and cultures. The mechanism of the entire operation is AIDS. AIDS is initially perceived as a fiendish intrusion in the lives of gay men. It is nonetheless co-opted from a hetero-relational discourse that reads it as the final wages of sin and of a social, psychological, and physical unnaturalness tantamount to death and is subsequently transfigured, not simply through the process of homographesis, but through an act of connivance that suspends difference into the dynamic of homo-relationality. In the process the heteros (the humans) momentarily disappear and only the homos (the birds) remain. This in fact is the final consequence of the deconstruction of Spanish history undertaken by Goytisolo in his "trilogy of treason." By reappropriating the ideology of blood through which Christian Spain was forged and present-day heterosexism is maintained, Goytisolo generates a new homo-praxis.[13]

Goytisolo revindicates both the ethnic (Semitic) other of Hispanic history as well as the gay male in the context of AIDS, granting him supreme value at a time when little is to be had. He goes so far as to convert his struggle into the archetypal human quest for dignity, freedom, and life. He views him, however ironically, as Christlike in his martyrdom and godlike in his triumph over affliction. Yet it must be emphasized, regardless of his reading of the texts (of San Juan de la Cruz and of AIDS as it is currently configured), that though the disease can be made to shatter the constructs of an alienated textual subject, it destroys life itself, *even* if this life is conceivable solely within the structures of a discourse. Indeed, when all is said and written, AIDS remains and people continue to die. Here, then, is the limitation of this kind of writing: it brings us to a dream and it ends. We are thus left to assume the practical tasks of living in a world of AIDS. Perhaps, having been infected by the radical sexual discourse of Goytisolo's homobiography, we are better equipped to do so.

Conclusion
Reflections on the Hispanic Homograph and the Homo Body

In the homobiography of Goytisolo, as in the gay and queer autobiographies heretofore analyzed, the body is the primary locus of textualization. It is on the body that sameness and difference are inscribed and described, and it is as a homograph that the homo body first becomes visible. AIDS has transformed the entire project of homographesis into a life and death struggle, though as the "history of homosexuality" so poignantly proves, the stakes have always been excruciatingly high. Homographesis, as evidenced through the life writing of Roig, Goytisolo, Gil de Biedma, Villena, Moix, and Almodóvar, is not a uniform operation and can be inflected so as to produce distinct kinds of homographs. Gay autobiography inscribes the homo in opposition to the hetero, but as the autobiographies of Roig, Goytisolo, and Gil de Biedma reveal, the inscribed homo is inexorably hetero-ized insofar as it exists solely in relation to what it is not. Queer autobiography interjects difference within the same/different binary in an attempt to resist the constraints of identity altogether. Villena, Moix, and Almodóvar all recognize the overdeterminism of identity, but as queer life writers they make it their prerogative to perform various identities and never take any of them too seriously. Homobiography, as a third instance of the homograph, is less concerned with the dynamics of hetero-relationality and aims to generate neither an individual essence nor a solo performance but a multiplicity of praxes, each with a common end. I have used these three taxonomies (gay, queer, and homo) as a means of elucidating both the possibilities as well as the limitations of the Hispanic homograph, but I must reiterate that they are at best provisional efforts to re-represent Spanish gender and sexuality. As products of homographesis, the meanings they inscribe are themselves subject to description, even if, as in the case of the queer, meaning is no more than an unloading of meaning. As the "different from the different," the queer, like the gay, is also a relational figure, as is the homo-act itself, which remains within the gravitational field of hetero-relationality and is eventually other-directed regardless of its fleeting realization of the homo-group. If I have shown a preference for this latter paradigm, it is simply because of its more explicit endeavor to achieve community.

The body, nonetheless, is the material of homographesis, and it is through its representation that the texts of Roig, Goytisolo, Gil de Biedma, Villena, Moix, and Almodóvar find their logic. According to the model of Smith, "the body is not to be identified with the individual or self. . . . [It] goes beyond experience (because it admits determinants unknown to the empirical subject); but it falls short of transcendence (because it admits no essence beyond or within itself)" (*The Body Hispanic* 10).[1] The body is thus a materiality whose meaning is never fixed, even despite the relative uniformity of the meanings ascribed to it. Each of the six Hispanic writers of this study, for example, discovers the body through a prior mediation of the other, and in each case this mediation functions to equate him with the negative element in a binary opposition intended to corroborate a positive value of masculinity that he is determined to lack: strength, courage, steadfastness, honesty, productiveness, moral fiber, health, the right to life, and so forth. As manifested through the AIDS writing of Goytisolo, the homo body, in its most extreme hetero-ized incarnation, is not only defined as the qualitative contrary of the straight-male body; it is denied ontological status entirely. Its invasion by a "foreign body," that is, its acquisition of the fatal deficiency through which organic unity is undone, is conflated with a sexual act through which the essence of homosexuality is seen to pass from mere potentiality into being. The realization of homosexuality is therefore made synonymous with self-annihilation, and in the end AIDS is construed as the final truth of the "homosexual body."[2]

In the essay "The Spectacle of AIDS," Watney defines the "homosexual body" as the absolute other with whom all identification is refused. It is his contention that the "homosexual body" can be posited only in a "transitive mode" (when the self is identified in a relation of difference from the other)

or, as I have suggested, hetero-relationally. AIDS, he argues, is currently uti-
lized as the preeminent instrument for rationalizing the impossibility of the
"homosexual body" and of homosexuality in general and serves as a warning
to all of the dire consequences of ever thinking otherwise. This manipulation of AIDS persists even after the death of the gay-male-with-AIDS, at
which time the project of heterosexism is carried to its relentless and grim
conclusion:

> The "homosexual body" . . . must be publicly seen to be humiliated, thrown
> around in zip-up plastic bags, fumigated, denied burial, lest there be any ac-
> knowledgment of the slightest sense of loss. Thus the "homosexual body"
> continues to speak after death, not as a *memento mori,* but as its exact reverse,
> for a life that must at all costs be seen to have been devoid of value, unregret-
> ted, unlamented, and — final indignity — effaced into a mere anonymous
> statistic. The "homosexual body" is "disposed of", like so much rubbish, like
> the trash it was in life. (*Practices of Freedom* 54)

If this is the picture of the "homosexual body" under the regime of heterosexuality, it is no surprise that representations of the homo body figure so
prominently in gay male life writing and that such tremendous efforts are
undertaken to remake both the body and the world that forms its condition.

The text of Villena is perhaps the most explicit with regard to the dynamics of homographesis and the writing of the homo body. As I indicate in the
analysis of *Ante el espejo,* Villena is inscribed with the essence of alterity
when his classmates, on orders from the patriarchal figure of the schoolmas-
ter, actually write on paper their reading of his body. In this instance the homograph begins as a collection of essays. The recollection of its inception by
the mature Villena is specifically a rewriting, by a particular writer, of a plurality of texts that derive from a long line of others and institutionalized
praxes, including the pupils, the schoolteacher, the Francoist educational
system, the Spanish class structure, and Hispanic machismo. In this polyse-
mous passage from *Ante el espejo* Villena insists that he would never conform
to the implicit demand of his peers to be the same as them and that he would
actively embody the difference that they had ascribed to him: "Nunca pensé
en ser diferente" (58) [I never thought of being different (trans. mine)], that
is, different from his already established difference. Rather, he would *be* his

difference in the form of an essence. His logic, however, betrays the descriptive thrust of the homograph. Not only can he conceive of difference solely in relation to its contrary, but he is also presumably indifferent to the other and therefore to the whole process of hetero-relationality through which difference arises in the first place: "nunca pensé en ser diferente, pensé que — en general — aquellos niños no tenían, para mí, interés ninguno" (58) [I never thought of being different, I thought that in general those boys were, for me, of no interest whatsoever (trans. mine)]. This indifference is not an essence but a performance, and through it the contours of the same/different binary begin to dissolve. Yet it is enacted by the camp/aristocrat in an effort to realize the "presencia lejana" as a means of survival in an alien and hostile environment. For this reason it is a solitary gesture that ultimately fails to engage the other or lead to the possibility of homo-relationality.

In the Villena homograph, the homo body is inherently hetero-ized insofar as its sameness is tantamount to its difference from the different. In the homographs of Goytisolo, Gil de Biedma, and Almodóvar, the homo body is similarly represented as the primary site of the discursive tensions of inscription and description: when Goytisolo is bashed by the Moroccan and Gil de Biedma and Goytisolo's queer San Juan de la Cruz are stricken with disease (their writing will henceforth continue to reflect the workings of sameness and difference while striving to counter its devastating effects through fantasies of an epic siege, poetic memory, and the divine word) or when Almodóvar is shown to have stocky legs (it is in that moment, after all, that he establishes complicity with Oscar Wilde and crystallizes the anti-essentialist and queer trajectory of his own creative career). Roig and Moix likewise reveal the structuration of the homograph through explicit representations of the body.

In *Todos los parques no son un paraíso,* Roig recounts a disastrous love affair with an Englishman named Ronald. On the night they meet, Ronald informs Roig that he bears a striking resemblance to Toulouse-Lautrec. Since Roig knows nothing of the artist, he goes the next day to the book department of Selfridges, where he locates a volume containing his picture. Herein he discovers his own image for the other: absurd, pathetic, and sad (136), which he accepts as definitive. Needless to say, this all bodes ill for his future relationship with Ronald. What is more, it discloses a passivity on the part of Roig vis-à-vis the other (both gay and straight) that will culminate at the end of his autobiographical enterprise with his agonized self-definition as a "despicable little man." Roig is never more than what he is told he is, and his life writing is frozen in the negative moment of homographesis — when the homo is inscribed, by the unwitting gay life writer, in all its negativity.

In a very different context, Moix recalls how during a period of childhood his classmates taunted him with the epithet "Dumbo" on account of his ele-phantlike ears. His initial reaction to their jeers was one of shame, and for a time he walked with his eyes riveted to the ground lest he be forced to face their mocking glares. Yet unlike Roig, he took it upon himself to reconfigure the negative identity with which he had been endowed. This was actually not so difficult. As any child imbued with Disney fiction knows, Dumbo was a hero who saved his poor mother from prison; and as maybe only a child like Moix would notice, he was also always accompanied by "un amigo muy bueno, un ratoncito sabiondo y picarón que le aconsejaba, lo guiaba y nunca lo dejó solo" (*El cine de los sábados* 324) [a very good friend, a know-it-all and cunning little mouse who advised him, guided him, and never left him alone (trans. mine)]. Moix therefore succeeded in using his cultural fic-tions as an instrument for both rescribing his body as heroic and envisioning reciprocity with the other. (It is at this point that he actually begins thinking of how he will one day meet his own Pepito Grillo, or Jiminy Cricket.) Both he and Roig, then, were told that they had "bad bodies," but in the end they made radically different choices regarding the way in which they would live and write their similar destinies.

Though there is no final word to be had on the body or on the meaning of sexuality as represented in these various homographic texts, it is nevertheless possible to trace a trajectory toward a kind of writing that is gay affirmative but that manages to avoid the all too obvious traps and shortcomings that characterize rigorous gay essentialism and uninformed queer performativ-ity. As a concluding example of this kind of writing, I would like to cite from a poem of Gil de Biedma. Gil de Biedma never wrote of his actual experience of AIDS, but his poetic writing, like his memoir, is mediated by the experi-ence of illness, and as a result he is perhaps somewhat more intent than oth-ers to assert a bios, on the site of the body, and in conjunction with the other. In a passage from the piece "Un cuerpo es el mejor amigo del hombre" ["A Body Is a Man's Best Friend"], he writes:

Las horas no han pasado, todavía,
y está mañana lejos igual a un arrecife
que apenas yo distingo.
     Tú no sientes
cómo el tiempo se adensa en esta habitación
con la luz encendida, como está fuera el frío
lamiendo los cristales . . . Qué deprisa,
en mi cama esta noche, animalito,
con la simple nobleza de la necesidad,
mientras que te miraba, te quedaste dormido.
Así pues, buenas noches.   (*Longing* 90)

[The hours aren't over, not yet,
and tomorrow's as far away
as a reef I can barely make out.
     You don't notice
how thickly time is growing in this room
with the lamp glowing, how the chill
is outside licking at the windowpanes. . . .
How quickly, little creature, you fell asleep
in my bed tonight with the easy nobility
born of necessity while I studied you.
So good night then.   (*Longing* 91)]

I do not want to linger, at this point, over what is self-evident: a dialogical structure intended to represent the poet and a lover as well as the poet and himself, as the object of a look, or as the Nolan translation puts it, of an act of "study" that can be taken as an autobiographical gesture that is now drawing to a close. Of significance is the image of the "animalito," a body divested of "human" essences (which in the case of the homo-body are almost always "dehumanizing"), save that of the nobility of its needs — needs consubstantial with the body but not reducible to the discursive structures that aim to delimit and control the body. The fundamental binary opposition of homographesis remains, namely, that of the inside/out. What is more, the inside is being penetrated by the outside, and time or the chill (and in the end death itself) will eventually congeal the provisional space herein projected. There is, nonetheless, a certain indifference to this fact, marked by the gaze as it turns away from the windowpanes, the site of specularity through which the hetero-relational structure of the inside/out is consti-tuted as such, and toward the homo body. The gaze of the Gil de Biedma po-etic voice, like that of San Juan de la Cruz "a vista de las aguas" [at the sight of the waters], is darkened as it slips from the discursive ken into a space that eludes inscription. This space is none other than the homo body revindi-cated, albeit somewhat ironically since it is now in a sense an "unknown" body, though conceivably with a new lease on life, as the final verse of the Gil de Biedma poem suggests, "por lo desconocido" (90) ["because a perfect stranger" (91)]. A body, of course, is never really "unknown," and certainly not a "perfect" stranger, but rather, as the practice of the Hispanic homo-graph has shown, an open-ended enterprise. The demonstration of this open-endedness in fact stands as the major accomplishment of the six writ-ers of this study and marks an auspicious point of departure for future les-bian and gay Spanish life writers.

Introduction

1. Major studies of lesbian and gay Hispanic and Latin American writing include Bergmann and Smith, Foster, and Smith, *Laws*. In the latter Smith specifically addresses the issue of gay Spanish autobiography.

2. The Hungarian Karl Maria Kertbeny coined the terms "homosexual" and "heterosexual." He is known to have used them privately in 1868. In 1869 he used the word "homosexuality" publicly in an anonymous pamphlet opposing the adoption of an "unnatural fornication" law for the unifed German state. The word "heterosexuality" did not appear in public discourse until eleven years later. See Katz 52–54.

3. Significant constructionist analyses of gay sexuality include those of Adam, D'Emilio, Halperin, Kinsman, and Weeks. Epstein assesses some of the shortcomings of constructionism. For a concise discussion of the essentialist/constructionist debate, see Fuss, *Essentially Speaking,* chap. 6.

4. Though the notion of a discrete homosexual identity did not exist in early modern Spain, Carrasco nevertheless suggests that certain codes of speech and feminine comportment among males point to the presence of a "homosexual ghetto" (135).

5. I base my understanding of hegemony on the work of Kinsman, who sees in Gramsci's model a means of theorizing not only the "narrow, economically defined notions of class relations" (32) but also the structures of race, gender, and heterosexuality.

6. In *El beso de la mujer araña* [*Kiss of the Spider Woman*], the character Valentín expresses an intuition of homo-relationality when, in the prison-cell vortex of a regime of political terror, he declares: "Aquí nadie oprime a nadie" (206) ["Here no one oppresses the other" (202)].

7. With regard to Mexican life writing, Woods points out that the memoir, with its focus on a public rather than a private life, has been the preferred autobiographical mode since the chroniclers first began practicing it in the sixteenth century.

8. The most recent comprehensive studies of Hispanic autobiography are Molloy's *At Face Value* and Fernández's *Apology to Apostrophe.* For Spanish autobiography, see also Goetz, Levisi, Pope, and Rosenberg, as well as the essays collected by Spadaccini and Talens, the special issue of *Anthropos* 125 (1991), *L'autobiographie en Espagne,* and *Ecrire sur soi en Espagne.*

9. Obviously, numerous gay and lesbian life writers have written through a "heterosexual drag," and Renza thus speaks of "homosexual autobiographers or autobiographical works like Whitman's or Genet's, written in the immediate context of heterosexual 'others' and disguised as such for the writing self by their socially privy ('in drag') pronominal references" (290).

10. In his critique of Sedgwick, Van Leer challenges the notion that the coming-out experience constitutes the organizing metaphor of gay autobiography (126).

11. Though the word "gay" entered the Catalán language from Provence before its appearance in English, its use in Catalán and Castilian to indicate "homosexual" is thought to have derived from English usage. Boswell nevertheless suggests that the Catalán "gai" might have originally signified same-sex desire. He comments on the intriguing parallel between "gai" and the Catalán "gaiol" for lover, as well as the Castilian "gaya" and older English "gay" to mean female prostitutes or the lifestyles of their male partners (*Christianity* 43n6). Perriam comments on the recent introduction into Spain of the term "queer," as well as the effort on the part of certain Spanish gays to reclaim the word "maricón" (*Desire and Dissent* 11).

12. For a partial English translation of the *Manifiesto,* see Likosky. For further discussion of lesbian and gay Spanish history and politics, see Enríquez and Mirabet i Mullol.

13. Sedgwick sees in homosociality a potential not only for homosexual desire but also for various forms of male bonding as well as homophobia.

14. For a more extensive discussion of *Heraclés,* see Mayhew. For a brief discussion of the autobiographical aspects of Gil-Albert's writing, see Asiaín Ansorena.

15. Homoeroticism figures prominently in European *fin-de-siècle* aestheticism, but as Gil de Biedma points out, it is curiously absent from the writing of the Generation of 1898 and from Spanish modernism in general (Swansey and Enríquez 214).

16. For studies of gay themes in the writings of Lorca and Cernuda, see Allen, Binding, Eisenberg, Romero, Sahuquillo Vásquez, Thomas, Velázquez Cueto, and Walsh.

17. More recent gay Spanish poets (in addition to Gil de Biedma and Villena) include Alejandro Céspedes, Pepe Espaliu, and Jordi Petit. Much of their poetry is explicitly autobiographical. Petit's collection *De hombre a hombre* casts his life experience in the political context of the immediate post-Franco period.

18. Gil de Biedma alleges that the theme of sterility that characterizes the Lorquian representation of love results from his assimilation of a peasant-proprietor sensibility that sees in reproduction its only means of survival (Swansey and Enríquez 207–8).

19. For discussions of the autobiographical aspects of Cernuda's writing, see

Caro Valverde and Romera Castillo. Eutimio Martín analyzes an unpublished autobiographical text of Lorca.

20. Perhaps the first record of a "gay" Spanish voice is to be found not in a literary text but in the oath of "blood-brotherhood" sworn by Pedro Didaz and Munio Vandilaz of Celanova in the year 1031. Though such pledges reveal homosociality, their emphasis on the domestic and economic aspects of the relationship adds weight to the argument of John Boswell that they are in fact instances of same-sex matrimony (see Boswell, *Same-Sex Unions* 257; Hinojosa 16n2).

Chapter One: Antonio Roig

1. For a discussion of the relationship of diary writing to gay sexuality, see Didier 107.

2. Exile as a theme in Spanish life writing can be traced to the autobiography of Joseph Blanco White. Gay life writers often describe a sense of inner exile in their homelands that is overcome only through a self-imposed exile abroad. For a discussion of the orientalist aspects of gay European configurations of the foreign, see Boone. For a discussion of the theme of exile in Spanish Civil War autobiographies, see Ugarte, *Shifting Ground*.

3. Translations of passages from the three Roig texts are mine.

4. In the case of Goytisolo, Castilian, rather than Catalán, was always the dominant language in his life, constituting a priori his linguistic and cultural condition: "Decir que no elegí la lengua sino que fui elegido por ella sería el modo más simple y correcto de ajustarme a la verdad" (*Coto vedado* 37) ["To say that I did not choose the language but that I was chosen by it would be the simplest way of conforming to the truth" (*Forbidden Territory* 29)].

5. Roig mistakenly compares his desire to confront the father figure with that of Kafka, whose childhood dynamics were altogether different.

6. This passage, and in particular the nineteenth-century designation "homosexual," does not appear as such in the writings of Paul. For an analysis of biblical references to same-sex relations, see Boswell, *Christianity*.

7. Roig asserts that for him the most moving scene in all literature occurs in *Crime and Punishment* when the murderer, Raskolnikov, kneels before the prostitute, Sonia, and exclaims: "Me arrodillo ante el sufrimiento humano" (*Variaciones* 182) [I kneel before human suffering]. For Roig this sentence constitutes the entire "gospel" of his life. In reading Dostoyevsky, he seems to equate the murderer with his Orestian persona and the prostitute with what he envisions as the martyred gay male. The passage is significant because it suggests, despite Roig's reverence for suffering, a distancing from the prostituted and feminized gay male.

8. By Roig's critics I mean those gay Spanish readers, mentioned in *Vidente,* who criticized *Parques* immediately after its publication.

9. Elsewhere Roig indicates a desire to vindicate nature, although the voice of nature, as he points out, "tarde o temprano siempre se venga" (*Variaciones* 217) [sooner or later always avenges itself]. This comment is highly ironic since it is precisely nature, as defined by the heterosexist ideology of the church and society, that ultimately avenges itself. Roig's autobiography thus continues to reveal the danger of attempting to justify gay sexuality through a vocabulary designed to repress it.

10. A similar sentiment is expressed by Unamuno in his autobiographical piece *Cómo se hace una novela* [How to make a novel], when he asserts that because of the alienation of the writing-self in the written text, "la literatura no es más que muerte" (*Autobiografía* 912) [literature is no more than death (trans. mine)].

Chapter Two: Juan Goytisolo

1. Goytisolo's anti-essentialism is in fact suggestive of an existentialist worldview (see Ugarte, *Trilogy of Treason* 50). However, to the extent that Goytisolo seeks an inherent gay identity, his autobiographical undertaking runs counter to the Sartrean notion that consciousness, though irreducible to language, is itself a species of nothingness.

2. The "trilogy of treason" includes *Señas de identidad* [Marks of identity], *Reivindicación del Conde don Julián* [The revindication of Count don Julian], and *Juan sin tierra* [Juan the landless].

3. Goytisolo's position is reminiscent of that of Unamuno, with whom ironically he feels little affinity. Unamuno begins *Cómo se hace una novela* with a declaration surprisingly similar to that of Goytisolo (*Autobiografía* 857).

4. Despite the presence of these traditional autobiographical features, Schulman argues that the thrust of *Coto vedado* is inherently nonchronological (56–57). Other critics of the Goytisolo autobiographies (in addition to those cited elsewhere in this chapter) include Dehennin, Loureiro, Moreiras-Menor, Navajas, Plaza, and Pope, "Theory and Contemporary Autobiographical Writing."

5. In his autobiography, *El pez en el agua: Memorias* [A Fish in the water: Memoirs], Vargas Llosa writes that he himself was a parricide, seeking to purge through writing not only his own abusive father but also various representatives of established power in Peruvian political and cultural life (346).

6. This theme is explored in current films about gay men, such as *My Own Private Idaho,* directed by Gus Van Sant.

7. Evans and Gamman clarify the distinction between the "look," which is asso-

ciated with the eye, and the "gaze," which is associated with the phallus. Whereas the former is a mode of perception, the latter is a mode of desire (16).

8. After the publication of *Coto vedado*, Goytisolo's brother Luis challenged certain of his statements about their grandfather and father. For his comments, see *Investigaciones y conjeturas de Claudio Mendoza*. For an analysis of the polemic between the two brothers, see Díaz-Migoyo.

9. Goytisolo's personal view of gay sexuality is fully clarified in adulthood through his platonic relationship with Genet. Pope discusses this relationship in "La hermandad del crimen."

10. Throughout this episode, the alienating look of Lucho is opposite in its function to the look of reciprocity discerned by the Franco-Argentine autobiographer Héctor Bianciotti during his first adolescent infatuation with another male: "I feel someone's gaze alight on me. One of the older boys is standing off on one side. I begin to tingle all over. I manage to look up; our eyes meet and we stare at each other for a few seconds: I as if in fear, he as if in recollection, and suddenly he is already inviting me into our secret" (133).

11. The term "Sotadic Zone" was coined by the nineteenth-century British commentator Richard Burton to designate a vast region comprising North Africa and the Arabian peninsula in which, he argues, the practice of sodomy is "popular and endemic" (qtd. in Boone 91). Goytisolo frequently invokes the image of the Sotadic Zone when referring to his own sexual ideal.

12. Labanyi contends that Goytisolo is actually less concerned in his autobiographies with giving a voice to gay men than to the various women in his past who have been silenced through patriarchy (216).

Chapter Three: Jaime Gil de Biedma

1. It was in an interview with Federico Campbell that Gil de Biedma made the famous statement: "En mi poesía no hay más que dos temas: el paso del tiempo y yo" (Campbell 249) [In my poetry there are only two themes: the passage of time and myself (trans. mine)].

2. Given the mortality rate of persons with AIDS, the groups primarily affected, and the negligence of government agencies in adequately responding to the crisis, Yingling argues that AIDS actually shares more with genocide than with plagues and epidemics of the past (306).

3. In the *Poemas póstumos* Gil de Biedma creates a character named Jaime Gil de Biedma, who dies and is eulogized in the poem "Después de la muerte de Jaime Gil de Biedma" [After the death of Jaime Gil de Biedma]. In this poem the poetic voice

announces: "Yo me salvé escribiendo / despúes de la muerte de Jaime Gil de Biedma" (In *Volver* [Return] 130) [I saved myself writing / after the death of Jaime Gil de Biedma (trans. mine)]. A similar sentiment is expressed at the end of the *Retrato*.

4. It should be noted, despite Gil de Biedma's tuberculosis, that the *Retrato* is not committed to issues related to disease, and thus differs radically in both tone and thrust from recent AIDS writing. With regard to AIDS testimonials Denneny writes: "This is not strong emotion recollected in tranquility [as is the *Retrato*]; these are reports from the combat zone. AIDS writing is urgent; it is engaged and activist writing; it is writing in response to a present threat; it is in it, of it, and aims to affect it. I can think of no good parallel for this in literary history" (46).

5. All translations are mine.

6. In reference to ontological sincerity, Sartre writes: "As soon as we posit ourselves as a certain being, by a legitimate judgment, based on inner experience or correctly deduced from *a priori* or empirical premises, then by that very positing we surpass this being" (*Being and Nothingness* 106).

7. The verse comes from the second segment of the poem *Voyages* (55).

8. Arias further comments on Gil de Biedma's rejection of the confessional mode in her analysis of the veiling of homoerotic desire in his poetry (116). She suggests that a similar analysis of the *Diario del artista seriamente enfermo* is in order (130). Such a task is clearly facilitated by the now published Philippine portion of the diary.

9. For a discussion of male sexual identity in the Latino and Latin American contexts, see not only Whitam and Mathy but also Almaguer, Lumsden, Murray, Paz, and Piedra. Hart also writes on gay sexuality in the Philippines.

10. A collection of photographs, interspersed throughout the *Diario del artista seriamente enfermo,* appears in the *Retrato* in the section between "Las islas de Circe" and "De regreso en Itaca." The first shot, taken just prior to Gil de Biedma's departure, shows him seated at a table in a nightclub looking at someone or something to his left. The focus is on Gil de Biedma, but as in all autobiographical discourse, the subject is uncontainable. Its structure is hetero-relational, and its meaning is forever deferred, beyond the ken of the observer.

11. The observation of Blanchard is significant in this context: "The autobiographer incapable of coinciding with the subject in the past can only articulate a vision which allows him to see himself in the past as in a painting. Without the power to alter the past he is restricted to seeing himself *qua* subject and deriving his feelings not from the performance of the act but from the representation of that performance" (106).

12. These changes perhaps relate to the experience with Juan Antonio and Gil

de Biedma's coming out, which, according to "Las islas de Circe," occurred during the summer of his twentieth year, and hence in 1950 (71).

13. The use of "otro cuerpo" in this passage is an obvious example of the veiling of homoeroticism discussed by Arias.

Chapter Four: Luis Antonio de Villena

An earlier version of this chapter appeared in *MLN* 110.2 (1995): 320–334 © 1995 by the Johns Hopkins University Press.

1. Winfield and Zimmermann discuss the autobiographical aspects of Villena's poetry. According to Winfield, the "I" of the early poems is masked (336), and even the more explicitly autobiographical pieces are veiled (339). A clear example of Villena's autobiographical poetics is "Mi retrato triste y suntuoso" (in *Poesía* 178–79) [My sad and sumptuous portrait]. For an overall discussion of the writing of Villena, see Perriam, *Desire and Dissent*.

2. *Ante el espejo* was published in 1982 with the subtitle *Memorias de una adolescencia* [Memoirs of an adolescence]. In the 1988 reprinting the subtitle was omitted. Citations are taken from the more recent edition, and translations are mine.

3. This is a feeling shared by numerous gay life writers. Monette begins his autobiography, *Becoming a Man: Half a Life Story,* with the declaration: "Everybody else had a childhood" (1). A similar attitude is expressed by Moix in the first volume of his memoirs (305).

4. One of the chief aims of Meyer's study is to reappropriate the queer praxis of camp that, in the wake of Sontag's 1964 article "Notes on 'Camp'" has been diffused within a popular culture that functions to reaffirm the dominant structures of sexuality: "Camp theorizing has languished since the 1960s when Sontag's appropriation banished the queer from the discourse, substituting instead an un-queer bourgeois subject under the banner of Pop" (10).

5. In "La tentación del orden" [The temptation of order] Villena identifies himself as an ex-supporter of the new right with a distrust of the traditional left. He adds: "Creo en la coherente incoherencia de los radicales. . . . Apuesto por la tentación del *desorden*. Por la sana, noble y eterna rebeldía" (13) [I believe in the coherent incoherence of radicals. . . . I bet on the temptation of *disorder.* On healthy, noble, and eternal rebellion (trans. mine)].

6. Villena characterizes homoeroticism as "una pulsión que no tiene destino práctico como la heterosexualidad que va orientada a la reproducción de la especie, y, por tanto, es más útil socialmente" (qtd. in Díaz 78) [a drive that has no practical goal, as does heterosexuality, which is oriented toward the reproduction of the spe-

cies and is therefore socially more useful (trans. mine)]. This comment in fact appears in the context of art. Villena relates gay sexuality to literature and the arts in general insofar as he discerns in it a ludic dimension not present in straight sexuality.

7. Memoirs of childhood and adolescence frequently reveal a nostalgia for an idyllic summer experience. Like Villena and Gil de Biedma, Chacel reflects in her autobiography on the summers of her past, and in describing an afternoon picnic in the country, she too recalls an intuition of unity and wholeness: "una especie de síntesis o quintaesencia de la realización, una emanación de la realidad, una cualidad suprema que daba consistencia al aire, a la luz, a las voces y las risas" (122) [a kind of synthesis or quintessence of realization, an emanation of reality, a supreme quality that gave consistency to the air, to the light, to the voices and the laughter (trans. mine)].

8. In contrast to Goytisolo, Villena imagines a relationship of equality with the exoticized "oriental" lover.

9. Villena develops images of the "south" (an avatar of European orientalism) in much of his poetry, including the book *Huir del invierno* [To flee from winter]. A piece from *Hymnica* [Hymnic], "Reinos de taifas" (in *Poesía* 176–77), shares its title with Goytisolo's second volume of memoirs. This poem places the Taifa kingdoms of Muslim Spain in an intermediate zone, between an oppressive Christian north and an Islamic south, where disunity makes possible the expression of a different kind of love.

10. In an interview with Díaz, Villena considers a somewhat more ascetic ending to his life story, though without abandoning his camp flare: "Después de haber vivido mil noches locas y mil cuerpos, a mí no me importaría nada terminar en una finquita del norte de Palencia leyendo a Schopenhauer con hábito franciscano. A lo mejor también me ponía una peluca Luis XV, para no dejar de ser lo que uno ha sido, pero echando de comer a las gallinas" (78) [After having lived a thousand mad nights and a thousand bodies, it wouldn't matter to me at all if I ended up on a little farm north of Palencia reading Schopenhauer in a Franciscan habit. Maybe I'd also put on a Louis XV wig, so as not to cease being who I had been, but also to feed the chickens in (trans. mine)].

11. The poetry of the period of *Ante el espejo* reveals a similar rejection of a fixed truth. See, for example, the series of poems *La muerte únicamente* [Death alone] in *Poesía*.

Chapter Five: Terenci Moix

1. *El cine de los sábados* covers the period of Moix's childhood, whereas *El beso de Peter Pan* focuses on his adolescent years up to the age of twenty-one. The first vol-

ume shares its title with a poem by the Spanish poet and autobiographer Antonio Martínez Sarrión (52). In the second, Moix not only evokes the title of *El beso de la mujer araña* but like Puig he also uses the image of the kiss to elucidate the relationship of popular cinema to the gay male spectator. In an introductory note to *El beso de Peter Pan* Moix announces three future installments of his autobiography: *La edad de un sueño «pop»* [The age of a pop dream], *El misterio del amor* [The mystery of love], and *Entrada de artistas* [Entrance of artists]. All five will fall under the general title *El Peso de la Paja* [The weight of straw], the name of the plaza in Barcelona where his childhood home was located. Parenthetical references in my text refer to *El beso de Peter Pan*. Translations are mine.

2. The term "gay gaze" first appeared in "When the Gaze Is Gay," the title of a section of *Film Comment* devoted to the representation of gays and lesbians in Hollywood cinema.

3. Moix was in fact born "Ramón Moix Meseguer" and uses "Terenci Moix" as a pen name. I will follow his practice of referring to his childhood and adolescent personae as Ramón.

4. According to Russo, the film *Rebel without a Cause* depicts a quasi-homosexual in the character played by Sal Mineo (109). Moix found this film less appealing than *East of Eden* because of its violence. He indicates, moreover, that it was withheld for several years from the Spanish screen by censors who feared its deleterious effects on Spanish youth (141). In his case, however, the seemingly more innocent *East of Eden* was to have a far greater impact.

5. Moix discusses at some length the film *Tea and Sympathy*. When he saw it as an adolescent, he viewed the character Tom as gay and identified with him, only to feel betrayed when he was "cured" of his "affliction" through a sexual experience with an older woman (166–67). Russo explains that the film did not explicitly deal with gay sexuality, since given the restrictions of the Production Code in effect at the time homoeroticism could not be represented and hence did not officially exist in Hollywood. Rather, the film portrays Tom as a "sissy," though as Russo writes, "*Tea and Sympathy* . . . confirms what the creators and portrayers of sissies have always sought to deny, that the iconography for sissies and for sexual deviates is the same and that the one has come to *mean* the other" (113). Thus, though early Hollywood films were ostensibly silent with regard to gay sexuality, they nevertheless sought to contain and ultimately eliminate it.

6. It seems likely, given the description of Peter Pan in *El beso de Peter Pan*, that Moix first encountered the character in the Disney film. This version of the Peter Pan narrative in fact highlights his masculinity while presenting the female characters in an exaggeratedly sexist light. Tinkerbell, for example, is so jealous of Wendy that she attempts to kill her. The response of the mermaids is similar. Peter, in con-

trast, is uninterested in the love of women, and his primary passion remains his un-explained rivalry with Captain Hook.

7. For a discussion of "blood brotherhood" as it relates to gay sexuality in Christian European history, see Boswell, *Same-Sex Unions.*

8. As Rose clarifies, the concept of origins is particularly problematical in the case of Peter Pan. Although the character first appeared in *The Little White Bird,* a theatrical version of his adventures was produced twenty-four years before Barrie actually wrote the play. What is considered the children's classic hence depends on a number of writers, and according to Rose the subsequent reworkings of the text are as significant as the ostensible source.

9. The name of this utopia is ambiguous. In Spanish, Nunca Jamás suggests a place that once existed but that has forever ceased to be, that is, the land of "never-more." In English three designations are used: Never Land, Never Never Land, and Never Never Never Land. The first and the third signify timelessness. The second, through the use of the double negation, indicates a place that has always existed (never never = ever) but that has heretofore been invisible. Moix renders it visible precisely through his queer gaze.

10. The culture of Moix's youth was limited primarily to popular cinema, movie magazines, and comic books. As a sort of autodidact (when he was thirteen his parents decided that he should attend a trade school rather than pursue an academic degree in preparation for the university), he eventually acquired "high" literary and cinematic tastes. It is through his reading of "low culture," however, that he expresses his greatest creativity. This, in keeping with the analysis of Fiske, might be explained at least in part by the very shallowness of "low culture" texts: "Conventionality and superficiality not only keep production costs down, they also open the text up to productive reading strategies" (109). A "high culture" text, on the other hand, often requires readers to decipher rather than generate meanings and can even work "to exclude those who have not the cultural competence [the undereducated Ramón] (or the motivation) to decode it on its own terms" (109).

11. Moix sees his uncle Cornelio (a pseudonym surely attributed to him by Ramón in an effort to equate him with the actor Cornel Wilde) and his lover Alberto as positive gay role models. Of his childhood friends, the so-called Niño Rico [Rich Boy] was significant insofar as he was the first to ascribe to Ramón the label "maricón" when the latter tentatively expressed his affection for him. The word fell on Ramón like a curse and a mark of shame, and it is with irony and bitterness that Moix describes in *El cine de los sábados* his surprise upon discovering years later that El Niño Rico was himself actually gay.

12. Elsewhere, Moix insists: "YO NO HABIA TENIDO INFANCIA" (*El cine de los sábados* 305) [I NEVER HAD A CHILDHOOD (trans. mine)]. Nevertheless, in this and

other moments with Roberto he reveals the spontaneity and exhilaration of a child, engaging in a playful behavior that is not an apprenticeship for adulthood but is rather an affirmation of freedom and an act of rebellion. His conception of play is in fact suggestive of Nietzsche's "gay science" and Sartre's rejection of the "spirit of seriousness."

13. Gore Vidal scripted and Willy Wyler directed this version of *Ben-Hur.* In his memoirs, Vidal explains at some length how he chose to read the original text as a tale of homoerotic love and how this might have negatively affected Wyler's career (301–7). His comments to Wyler and Sam Zimbalist regarding the relationship of Ben-Hur and Messala were in fact surprisingly similar to those of Roberto to Ramón. Vidal recalls: "I . . . told them that Ben Hur and Messala had been boyhood lovers. But Ben Hur, under the fierce Palestinian sun and its jealous god, has turned straight as a die while Messala, the decadent gentile, had remained in love with Ben and wanted to take up where they had left off" (304). (Russo also cites this conversation [76–77].) Despite significant cultural differences, Vidal and Roberto thus queer the narrative in the same way.

14. This magical space is reminiscent of the rooms of both Melquíades in *Cien años de soledad* [One hundred years of solitude] and Carmen Martín Gaite in *El cuarto de atrás* [The back room], in that it is posited as the site wherein the text is generated. It also evokes the room in the pawnbroker's shop in *Fanny and Alexander,* where the young Bergman discovers his own alter ego and the source of his creative genius.

15. It should be noted that Ramón had several sexual experiences during adolescence, but like the encounter in the Cine Cervantes, none was particularly fulfilling.

Chapter Six: Pedro Almodóvar

1. Little attention has been paid to Almodóvar's writing. For a discussion of his film production, see Besas, Hopewell, Kinder, Smith (both *Laws* and *Desire Unlimited*), and Vernon and Morris.

2. For a discussion of the camp aesthetic of Almodóvar, see Pally.

3. In Spanish the word "patidifusa" means "astounded" or "flabbergasted." In the context of queer theory, it also suggests a diffuseness that resists the grounding of identity as well as the political immediacy (and often the efficacy) that paradigms of identity make possible.

4. According to Morris, in *Patty Diphusa,* as in *La ley del deseo,* the "confluence of camp and masochistic discourses is played out on a re/construction of the female body" (94).

5. In *Antes que anochezca* [Before night falls], the Cuban writer and autobiogra-

pher Reinaldo Arenas recounts the brutalization of Cuban gays under the early Castro regime.

Patty's fantasy is also reminiscent of the ending of *El beso de la mujer araña* when Valentín, under the influence of a drug, escapes violence by fantasizing an idyllic tropical setting. In contrast to Puig, who juxtaposes the discourses of the real and the imaginary, Almodóvar camps the entire world of the Patty Diphusa text and thus, to a certain degree, derealizes it.

6. As Goldhill writes with regard to ancient Greco/Roman texts, erotic desire occurs only to the extent that it is expressed discursively (11). In the *Daphnis and Chloe* of Longus, for example, it is not sufficient for Chloe to observe the nude body of Daphnis. For her to experience erotic desire, she must also describe it.

7. In *Laws of Desire,* Smith analyzes the self-referentiality of several of Almodóvar's films, including *Pepi, Luci, Bom, y otras chicas del montón* [Pepi, Luci, Bom, and other ordinary girls], *Entre tinieblas* [Dark habits], and *La ley del deseo* (168). In *Desire Unlimited,* he discusses the explicitly autobiographical aspects of *La ley del deseo* (79).

8. Morris discusses the mother figure in *La ley del deseo* in the context of the theory of masochism developed by Gilles Deleuze (91–92).

9. The dialogue between Patty and Pedro is reminiscent of the encounter between Unamuno and Augusto Pérez in *Niebla* [Mist]. Clearly, this text lacks the explicit sexual dynamics of *Patty Diphusa*. Yet interestingly enough, Unamuno's fictional narrator, Víctor Goti, feels obliged to reject the charge that *Niebla* is pornographic (49), perhaps on account of its unusual reworking of the gaze in the male/female and author/character relationships.

10. With regard to the self-referentiality of Almodóvar's films, Smith writes that "narrative is internalized as the object (not the means) of representation" (*Laws* 168). This is the case in the Patty Diphusa collection, where the text functions not so much as a means of achieving self-representation but rather as a reflection on and a disengagement from an already constituted representation of the self.

Chapter Seven: Juan Goytisolo with Birds of a Feather

1. Javier Escudero Rodríguez maintains that when Goytisolo wrote *Las virtudes del pájaro solitario,* he was overcome by an almost obsessive fear of AIDS (56). Goytisolo speaks of this fear in the article "El Cairo. La Ciudad de los Muertos" [Cairo. The City of the Dead].

2. A prime example of AIDS writing is the autobiography of Arenas. The Cuban Severo Sarduy also reflects on AIDS in the autobiographical essays "Explosion of Emptiness" and "A Wart on My Foot." For an extensive list of AIDS autobiogra-

phies, consult the annotated bibliography of Brooks and Murphy. For an analysis of AIDS life writing, see Chandler. For other examples of AIDS testimonials, see Preston.

3. This continued to be reaffirmed even in 1995 when, for example, the security personnel of the president of the United States, regardless of political motivation, chose to wear rubber gloves to receive gay visitors to the White House.

4. Though it is believed that San Juan de la Cruz wrote the treatise of the birds, no manuscript has ever been located. Goytisolo suggests that San Juan de la Cruz ate it when he was arrested by his enemies within the Carmelite Order and imprisoned. However, it is the opinion of Crisógono de Jesús Sacramentado, chief Sanjuanist biographer of this century, that the papers eaten at the time of the arrest dealt specifically with the reform movement of the discalced Carmelites (143).

5. For an analysis of the Muslim influences on Sanjuanist mysticism, see *San Juan de la Cruz y el Islam* [San Juan de la Cruz and Islam] by López Baralt, which Goytisolo acknowledges as one of various sources he consulted in preparation for *Las virtudes del pájaro solitario.*

6. Gay Hispanic poets often invoke Sanjuanist imagery in representing gay love as well as the "dark night" of AIDS. See Céspedes, Rodríguez Matos, and Sarduy.

7. As Levine indicates, Goytisolo obtained much of his information on the UMAP from this film (229).

8. For a discussion of gay sexuality and AIDS in Cuba, see Leiner.

9. Ruiz Lagos maintains that the origin of the Ben Sida figure is "Abu-l-Hasan Alí b. Ismail al-Mursí o al-Andalusí," known as "Ibn Sida, el Ciego" (214).

10. As Martín Morán points out, the Koran speaks of a "lenguaje de pájaros" as a means of communicating with the Divinity (28).

11. In San Juan de la Cruz mystical transformation is in fact expressed through the four primordial elements of earth, water, fire, and air.

12. This is but one of the numerous intertextual references to San Juan de la Cruz. The words echo the final stanza of the poem "Cántico espiritual" [Spiritual canticle]. See *Obras completas,* 441, 572.

13. *Las virtudes del pájaro solitario* is not without its critics. Smith, for example, argues that Goytisolo homogenizes difference and conflates, among various subalternate categories, both religious and sexual deviance. Yet if these are the same, he asks, then "do we not remain locked into the specular logic of the oppressors?" (*Representing the Other* 212). Smith further wonders what, if any, consolation persons with AIDS will derive from Goytisolo's representation of the disease. In depicting gays as "twittering in a gilded cage" (212), and more precisely by attempting "to transform physical misfortune into redemptive sacrifice" (212), Goytisolo, as Smith sees it, comes dangerously close "to parroting (rather than parodying) the forces of

oppression" (212) that he opposes. In her analysis of *La cuarentena* [The quarantine], in contrast, Levine works from the premise that the Goytisolo texts operate as parasites on what Smith calls the "host" text (214), to suggest that the reader is ultimately "infected" and politicized by his writing ("La escritura infecciosa de Juan Goytisolo" 96). For Smith, then, Goytisolo inadvertently reproduces dominant representations of homosexuality and AIDS as inscribed on the gay male body, whereas for Levine he manages to re-represent this body in a way that allows for a resituation on the part of readers within and in opposition to the "anti-discourses" (anti-gay-male, anti-female, anti-PWA, anti-Semitic, and so forth) of the "host" text.

Conclusion

1. For Butler, the materiality of the body is inseparable from the performativity of gender and from the heterosexual norms that function to regulate sexuality and constitute sex itself. See *Bodies That Matter* for the most thorough and incisive of the numerous cultural studies critiques of the body that have appeared in the wake of Foucault.

2. The elucidation of heterosexual ideology is surely facilitated by the fact that one of the primary modes of HIV transmission is anal sex, since this act has already been anathematized as the ultimate means through which the male body is dispossessed of the essence of masculinity and in a sense of its life. To consent to the "passive" role is hence perceived as a self-destructive gesture that the contraction of AIDS simply expedites.

Adam, Barry D. "Structural Foundations of the Gay World." *Comparative Study of Society and History* 27.4 (1985): 658–71.

———. *The Survival of Domination: Inferiorization and Everyday Life.* New York: Elsevier, 1978.

Allen, Rupert C. "Luis Cernuda: Poet of Gay Protest." *Hispanófila* 28.2 (1985): 61–78.

Almaguer, Tomás. "Chicano Men: A Cartography of Homosexual Identity and Behavior." In *The Lesbian and Gay Studies Reader.* Ed. Henry Abelove, Michèle Aina Barale, and David M. Halperin. New York: Routledge, 1993. 255–73.

Almodóvar, Pedro. *Patty Diphusa and Other Writings.* Trans. Kirk Anderson. Boston: Faber and Faber, 1992.

———. *Patty Diphusa y otros textos.* Barcelona: Anagrama, 1991.

Alonso, Ana María, and María Teresa Koreck. "Silences: 'Hispanics,' AIDS, and Sexual Practices." In *The Lesbian and Gay Studies Reader.* Ed. Henry Abelove, Michèle Aina Barale, and David M. Halperin. New York: Routledge, 1993. 110–26.

Arenas, Reinaldo. *Antes que anochezca: Autobiografía.* Barcelona: Tusquets, 1992.

Arias, Consuelo. "(Un)veiling Desire: Configurations of Eros in the Poetry of Jaime Gil de Biedma." *Anales de la Literatura Española Contemporánea* 18.1–2 (1993): 113–36.

Asiaín Ansorena, Alfredo. "La ilusión de referencialidad en la confesión autobiográfica: Juan Gil-Albert." In *Escritura autobiográfica: Actas del II seminario internacional del instituto de semiótica literaria y teatral Madrid, UNED, 1–3 de julio, 1992.* Ed. José Romera Castillo, Alicia Yllera, Mario García-Page, and Rosa Calvet. Madrid: Visor, 1993. 93–98.

Augustine, Saint. *The Confessions of Saint Augustine.* Trans. Sir Tobie Matthew. Rev. and introd. Dom Roger Hudleston. London: Burns and Oates, 1954.

L'autobiographie en Espagne: Actes du IIe colloque international de la Baume-les-Aix, 23–24–25 mai 1981. Etudes Hispaniques 5. Aix-en-Provence: Université de Provence, 1982.

Babuscio, Jack. "Camp and the Gay Sensibility." In *Camp Grounds: Style and Homosexuality.* Ed. David Bergman. Amherst: University of Massachusetts Press, 1993. 19–38.

Barrie, J. M. *The Little White Bird.* London: Hodder and Stoughton, 1902.

Bergman, David. Introduction. *Camp Grounds: Style and Homosexuality.* Ed. David Bergman. Amherst: University of Massachusetts Press, 1993. 3–16.

Bergmann, Emilie L., and Paul Julian Smith, eds. *¿Entiendes?: Queer Readings, Hispanic Writings.* Durham: Duke University Press, 1995.

Bersani, Leo. *Homos.* Cambridge, Mass.: Harvard University Press, 1995.

Besas, Peter. *Behind the Spanish Lens: Spanish Cinema under Fascism and Democracy.* Denver: Arden, 1985.

Bianciotti, Héctor. *What the Night Tells the Day.* Trans. Linda Coverdale. New York: New Press, 1995.

Binding, Paul. *Lorca: The Gay Imagination.* London: GMP, 1985.

Blanchard, Marc Eli. "The Critique of Autobiography." *Comparative Literature* 34.2 (1982): 97–115.

Blanco White, Joseph. *The Life of the Rev. Joseph Blanco White, Written by Himself; With Portions of His Correspondence.* 3 vols. Ed. John Hamilton Thom. London: John Chapman, 1845.

Boone, Joseph A. "Vacation Cruises; or, The Homoerotics of Orientalism." *PMLA* 110.1 (1995): 89–107.

Boswell, John. *Christianity, Social Tolerance, and Homosexuality: Gay People in Western Europe from the Beginning of the Christian Era to the Fourteenth Century.* Chicago: University of Chicago Press, 1980.

———. *Same-Sex Unions in Premodern Europe.* New York: Villard, 1994.

Brooks, Franklin, and Timothy F. Murphy. "Annotated Bibliography of AIDS Literature, 1982–91." In *Writing AIDS: Gay Literature, Language, and Analysis.* Ed. Timothy F. Murphy and Suzanne Poirier. New York: Columbia University Press, 1993. 321–39.

Burton, Richard, trans. and ed. The Book of the Thousand Nights and a Night: *A Plain and Literal Translation of the Arabian Nights Entertainments.* 10 vols. Burton Club ed. London: n.p., 1885–86.

Buss, Helen M. "*Bios* in Women's Autobiography." *a/b: Auto/Biography Studies* 10.1 (1995): 114–25.

Butler, Judith. *Bodies That Matter: On the Discursive Limits of "Sex."* New York: Routledge, 1993.

———. *Gender Trouble: Feminism and the Subversion of Identity.* New York: Routledge, 1990.

Campbell, Federico. *Infame turba.* Barcelona: Lumen, 1971.

Cañas, Dionisio. "Moral y máscara del canto." *El País* 12 Jan. 1990: 28.

Caro Valverde, María Teresa. "Yo de papel: El ejemplo de Luis Cernuda." In *Escritura autobiográfica: Actas del II seminario internacional del instituto de semiótica literaria y teatral Madrid, UNED, 1–3 de julio, 1992.* Ed. José Romera Castillo, Alicia Yllera, Mario García-Page, and Rosa Calvet. Madrid: Visor, 1993. 139–45.

Carrasco, Rafael. *Inquisición y represión sexual en Valencia: Historia de los sodomitas (1565–1785)*. Barcelona: Laertes, 1985.

Cernuda, Luis. *Poesía completa*. Barcelona: Seix Barral, 1974.

Céspedes, Alejandro. *La noche y sus consejos*. Granada: Genil, 1986.

Chacel, Rosa. *Desde el amanecer: Autobiografía de mis primeros diez años*. Madrid: Revista de Occidente, 1972.

Chandler, Marilyn. "Voices from the Front: AIDS in Autobiography." *a/b: Auto/Biography Studies* 6.1 (1991): 54–64.

Cohan, Steven, and Ina Rae Hark. Introduction. *Screening the Male: Exploring Masculinities in Hollywood Cinema*. Ed. Steven Cohan and Ina Rae Hark. New York: Routledge, 1993. 1–8.

Crane, Hart. *Complete Poems*. Ed. Brom Weber. Newcastle upon Tyne: Bloodaxe Books, 1984.

Crisógono de Jesús Sacramentado. *Vida de San Juan de la Cruz*. Ed. Matías del Niño Jesús. 11th ed. Madrid: Biblioteca de Autores Cristianos, 1982.

Curtin, John Claude. "Autobiography and the Dialectic of Consciousness." *International Philosophical Quarterly* 14.3 (1974): 343–46.

Dehennin, Elsa. "Relato en primera persona: Novela autobiográfica versus autobiografía. El caso de Juan Goytisolo." In *Homenaje al profesor Antonio Vilanova*. Ed. Adolfo Sotelo Vásquez and Marta Cristina Carbonell. Vol. 2. Barcelona: Departamento de Filología Española, Universidad de Barcelona, 1989. 149–61.

de Man, Paul. "Autobiography as De-Facement." *MLN* 94.5 (1979): 919–30.

D'Emilio, John. "Capitalism and Gay Identity." In *The Lesbian and Gay Studies Reader*. Ed. Henry Abelove, Michèle Aina Barale, and David M. Halperin. New York: Routledge, 1993. 467–76.

Denneny, Michael. "AIDS Writing and the Creation of a Gay Culture." In *Confronting AIDS through Literature: The Responsibilities of Representation*. Ed. Judith Laurence Pastore. Urbana: University of Illinois Press, 1993. 36–54.

Denning, Michael. "The End of Mass Culture." In *Modernity and Mass Culture*. Ed. James Naremore and Patrick Brantlinger. Bloomington: Indiana University Press, 1991. 253–68.

Derrida, Jacques. *The Ear of the Other: Otobiography, Transference, Translation*. Ed. Christie V. McDonald. Trans. Peggy Kamuf. New York: Schocken, 1985.

Díaz, Lola. "Luis Antonio de Villena, disfrazado de sí mismo." *Cambio 16* 719 (9–16 Sept. 1985): 76-78.

Díaz-Migoyo, Gonzalo. "La ajena autobiografía de los hermanos Goytisolo." *Anthropos* 125 (1991): 61–62.

Didier, Béatrice. *Le journal intime*. Paris: Presses Universitaires de France, 1976.

Dollimore, Jonathan. *Sexual Dissidence: Augustine to Wilde, Freud to Foucault.* Oxford: Clarendon, 1991.

Dostoyevsky, Fyodor. *Crime and Punishment: A Novel in Six Parts with Epilogue.* Trans. Richard Pevear and Larissa Volokhonsky. New York: Vintage, 1993.

Doty, Alexander. *Making Things Perfectly Queer: Interpreting Mass Culture.* Minneapolis: University of Minnesota Press, 1993.

Drukman, Steven. "The Gay Gaze; or, Why I Want My MTV." In *A Queer Romance: Lesbians, Gay Men, and Popular Culture.* Ed. Paul Burston and Colin Richardson. New York: Routledge, 1995. 81–95.

Dust, Patrick. "A Methodological Prolegomenon to a Post-Modernist Reading of Santa Teresa's Autobiography." In *Autobiography in Early Modern Spain.* Ed. Nicholas Spadaccini and Jenaro Talens. Minneapolis: Prisma Institute, 1988. 77–96.

Dyer, Richard. "Entertainment and Utopia." In *The Cultural Studies Reader.* Ed. Simon During. New York: Routledge, 1993. 271–83.

———. *The Matter of Images: Essays on Representations.* New York: Routledge, 1993.

———. "Rock — The Last Guy You'd Have Figured?" In *You Tarzan: Masculinity, Movies, and Men.* Ed. Pat Kirkham and Janet Thumim. New York: St. Martin's Press, 1993. 27–34.

Eakin, Paul John. *Fictions in Autobiography: Studies in the Art of Self-Invention.* Princeton: Princeton University Press, 1985.

Edelman, Lee. *Homographesis: Essays in Gay Literary and Cultural Theory.* New York: Routledge, 1994.

Eisenberg, Daniel. "Reaction to the Publication of the *Sonetos del amor oscuro.*" In *Homosexual Themes in Literary Studies.* Ed. Wayne R. Dynes and Stephen Donaldson. New York: Garland, 1992. 129–39.

Ellis, John. "On Pornography." In *The Sexual Subject: A Screen Reader in Sexuality.* Ed. John Caughie and Annette Kuhn. New York: Routledge, 1992. 146–70.

Enríquez, José Ramón, ed. *El homosexual ante la sociedad enferma.* Barcelona: Tusquets, 1978.

Epstein, Steven. "Gay Politics, Ethnic Identity: The Limits of Social Constructionism." *Socialist Review* 17.3–4 (1987): 9–54.

Escudero Rodríguez, Javier. *Eros, mística y muerte en Juan Goytisolo (1982–1992).* Almería: Instituto de Estudios Almerienses, Departamento de Arte y Literatura, 1994.

Espaliu, Pepe. *En estos cinco años (1987–1992).* Madrid: Estampa, 1993.

Evans, Caroline, and Lorraine Gamman. "The Gaze Revisited; or, Reviewing

Queer Viewing." In *A Queer Romance: Lesbians, Gay Men, and Popular Culture.* Ed. Paul Burston and Colin Richardson. New York: Routledge, 1995. 13–56.

Felski, Rita. "The Counterdiscourse of the Feminine in Three Texts by Wilde, Huysmans, and Sacher-Masoch." *PMLA* 106.5 (1991): 1094–1105.

Fernández, James D. *Apology to Apostrophe: Autobiography and the Rhetoric of Self-Representation in Spain.* Durham: Duke University Press, 1992.

———. "La novela familiar del autobiógrafo: Juan Goytisolo." *Anthropos* 125 (1991): 54–60.

Fiske, John. "Popular Discrimination." In *Modernity and Mass Culture.* Ed. James Naremore and Patrick Brantlinger. Bloomington: Indiana University Press, 1991. 103–16.

Foster, David William. *Gay and Lesbian Themes in Latin American Writing.* Austin: University of Texas Press, 1991.

Foucault, Michel. *Discipline and Punish: The Birth of the Prison.* Trans. Alan Sheridan. New York: Pantheon, 1977.

———. *The History of Sexuality, Volume 1: An Introduction.* Trans. Robert Hurley. New York: Pantheon, 1978.

Fuss, Diana. *Essentially Speaking: Feminism, Nature, and Difference.* New York: Routledge, 1989.

———. "Inside/Out." In *Inside/Out: Lesbian Theories, Gay Theories.* Ed. Diana Fuss. New York: Routledge, 1991. 1–10.

García Lorca, Federico. *The Public and Play without a Title: Two Posthumous Plays.* Trans. Carlos Bauer. New York: New Directions, 1983.

———. *El público y Comedia sin título: Dos obras teatrales póstumas.* Ed. R. Martínez Nadal and M. Lafranque. Barcelona: Seix Barral, 1978.

García Márquez, Gabriel. *Cien años de soledad.* Buenos Aires: Sudamericana, 1967.

Gibbon, Edward. *Memoirs of My Life.* Ed. Georges A. Bonnard. London: Nelson, 1966.

Giddens, Anthony. *The Constitution of Society: Outline of the Theory of Structuration.* Berkeley: University of California Press, 1984.

Gil-Albert, Juan. *Heraclés/Drama patrio.* Vol. 7 of *Obra completa en prosa.* Valencia: Institución Alfonso el Magnánimo, Diputación Provincial de Valencia, 1984. 12 vols. 1982–89.

Gil de Biedma, Jaime. *Diario del artista seriamente enfermo.* Barcelona: Lumen, 1974.

———. *Longing: Selected Poems.* Trans. James Nolan. San Francisco: City Lights, 1993.

———. *Retrato del artista en 1956.* Barcelona: Lumen, 1991.

———. *Volver.* Ed. Dionisio Cañas. Madrid: Cátedra, 1989.

Goetz, Rainer H. *Spanish Golden Age Autobiography in Its Context.* New York: Peter Lang, 1995.

Goldhill, Simon. *Foucault's Virginity: Ancient Erotic Fiction and the History of Sexuality.* Cambridge: Cambridge University Press, 1995.

Goytisolo, Juan. "El Cairo. La Ciudad de los Muertos." *El País Semanal* 8 Feb. 1987: 30–37, 60–64.

———. *Coto vedado.* Barcelona: Seix Barral, 1985.

———. *La cuarentena.* Madrid: Mondadori, 1991.

———. *En los reinos de taifa.* Barcelona: Seix Barral, 1986.

———. *Forbidden Territory: The Memoirs of Juan Goytisolo, 1931–1956.* Trans. Peter Bush. San Francisco: North Point, 1989.

———. *Juan sin tierra.* Barcelona: Seix Barral, 1975.

———. *Realms of Strife: The Memoirs of Juan Goytisolo, 1957–1982.* Trans. Peter Bush. San Francisco: North Point, 1990.

———. *Reivindicación del Conde don Julián.* Mexico City: Joaquín Mortiz, 1970.

———. *Señas de identidad.* Mexico City: Joaquín Mortiz, 1966.

———. *Las virtudes del pájaro solitario.* Barcelona: Seix Barral, 1988.

———. *The Virtues of the Solitary Bird.* Trans. Helen Lane. London: Serpent's Tail, 1991.

Goytisolo, Luis. *Investigaciones y conjeturas de Claudio Mendoza.* Barcelona: Anagrama, 1985.

Gusdorf, Georges. "Conditions and Limits of Autobiography." Trans. James Olney. In *Autobiography: Essays Theoretical and Critical.* Ed. James Olney. Princeton: Princeton University Press, 1980. 28–48.

Halperin, David M. *One Hundred Years of Homosexuality: And Other Essays on Greek Love.* New York: Routledge, 1990.

Haraway, Donna. "A Manifesto for Cyborgs: Science, Technology, and Socialist Feminism in the 1980s." *Socialist Review* 15.2 (1985): 65–107.

Hark, Ina Rae. "Animals or Romans: Looking at Masculinity in *Spartacus.*" In *Screening the Male: Exploring Masculinities in Hollywood Cinema.* Ed. Steven Cohan and Ina Rae Hark. New York: Routledge, 1993. 151–72.

Hart, Donn V. "Homosexuality and Transvestism in the Philippines: The Cebuan Filipino Bayot and Lakin-on." *Behavior Science Notes* 3.4 (1968): 211–48.

Hennessy, Rosemary. "Queer Theory, Left Politics." In *Marxism beyond Marxism.* Ed. Saree Makdisi, Cesare Casarino, and Rebecca E. Karl. New York: Routledge, 1996. 214–42.

Hinojosa, Eduardo de. "La fraternidad artificial en España." *Revista de Archivos, Bibliotecas y Museos* 3.9 (1905): 1–18.

Hopewell, John. *Out of the Past: Spanish Cinema after Franco.* London: British Film Institute, 1986.

Jackson, Earl, Jr. *Strategies of Deviance: Studies in Gay Male Representation.* Bloomington: Indiana University Press, 1995.

Juan de la Cruz, San. *Obras completas.* Ed. Lucinio Ruano de la Iglesia. 12th ed. Madrid: Biblioteca de Autores Cristianos, 1989.

Katz, Jonathan Ned. *The Invention of Heterosexuality.* New York: Plume/Penguin, 1996.

Kinder, Marsha. *Blood Cinema: The Reconstruction of National Identity in Spain.* Berkeley: University of California Press, 1993.

King, Thomas A. "Performing 'Akimbo': Queer Pride and Epistemological Prejudice." In *The Politics and Poetics of Camp.* Ed. Moe Meyer. New York: Routledge, 1994. 23–50.

Kinsman, Gary. *The Regulation of Desire: Sexuality in Canada.* Montréal: Black Rose Books, 1987.

Labanyi, Jo. "The Construction/Deconstruction of the Self in the Autobiographies of Pablo Neruda and Juan Goytisolo." *Forum for Modern Language Studies* 26.3 (1990): 212–21.

Lacan, Jacques. "The Meaning of the Phallus." In *Feminine Sexuality: Jacques Lacan and the* école freudienne. Ed. Juliet Mitchell and Jacqueline Rose. Trans. Jacqueline Rose. New York: Pantheon, 1982. 74–85.

Leiner, Marvin. *Sexual Politics in Cuba: Machismo, Homosexuality, and AIDS.* Boulder, Colo.: Westview Press, 1994.

Lejeune, Philippe. "Autobiographie et homosexualité en France au XIXe siècle." *Romantisme* 17.56 (1987): 79–94.

———. *On Autobiography.* Ed. Paul John Eakin. Trans. Katherine Leary. Minneapolis: University of Minnesota Press, 1989.

———. "Répertoire des autobiographies écrites en France au XIXe siècle (1789–1914). Section 4: Vies d'homosexuels." *Romantisme* 17.56 (1987): 95–100.

Levine, Linda Gould. "La escritura infecciosa de Juan Goytisolo: Contaminación y cuarentena." *Revista de Estudios Hispánicos* 28.1 (1994): 95–110.

———. "El papel paradójico del 'Sida' en *Las virtudes del pájaro solitario.*" In *Escritos sobre Juan Goytisolo: Actas del II seminario internacional sobre la obra de Juan Goytisolo:* Las virtudes del pájaro solitario. Ed. Manuel Ruiz Lagos. Almería: Instituto de Estudios Almerienses, 1990. 225–36.

Levisi, Margarita. *Autobiografías del Siglo de Oro: Jerónimo de Pasamonte, Alonso de Contreras, Miguel de Castro.* Madrid: Sociedad General Española de Librería, 1984.

Likosky, Stephan, trans. "Spain: Common Platform Authored by the Coordinated

Homosexual Liberation Fronts of the Spanish State (COFLHEE)." In *Coming Out: An Anthology of International Gay and Lesbian Writings*. Ed. Stephan Likosky. New York: Pantheon, 1992. 204–8.

López Baralt, Luce. *San Juan de la Cruz y el Islam: Estudio sobre las filiaciones semíticas de su literatura mística*. Mexico City: El Colegio de México; Río Piedras: Universidad de Puerto Rico, 1985.

Loureiro, Angel G. "Autobiografía del otro (Rousseau, Torres Villarroel, Juan Goytisolo)." *Siglo XX/Twentieth Century* 9.1–2 (1991–92): 71–94.

Lumsden, Ian. *Homosexuality, Society, and the State in Mexico*. Mexico City: Solediciones; Toronto: Canadian Gay Archives, 1991.

Mandel, Barrett J. "Full of Life Now." In *Autobiography: Essays Theoretical and Critical*. Ed. James Olney. Princeton: Princeton University Press, 1980. 49–72.

Mandrell, James. "Sense and Sensibility; or, Latent Heterosexuality and *Labyrinth of Passions.*" In *Post-Franco, Postmodern: The Films of Pedro Almodóvar*. Ed. Kathleen M. Vernon and Barbara Morris. Westport, Conn.: Greenwood, 1995. 41–57.

Martin, Biddy. "Lesbian Identity and Autobiographical Differences." In *Life/Lines: Theorizing Women's Autobiography*. Ed. Bella Brodzki and Celeste Schenck. Ithaca: Cornell University Press, 1988. 77–103.

Martín, Eutimio. "En torno a un texto autobiográfico (inédito) de Federico García Lorca." In *L'autobiographie en Espagne. Actes du IIe colloque international de la Baume-les-Aix, 23–24–25 mai 1981*. Etudes Hispaniques 5. Aix-en-Provence: Université de Provence, 1982. 227–59.

Martínez Sarrión, Antonio. *El centro inaccesible (Poesía 1967–1980)*. Madrid: Hiperión, 1981.

Martín Gaite, Carmen. *El cuarto de atrás*. Barcelona: Destino, 1978.

Martín Morán, José Manuel. "La escritura mística de Juan Goytisolo." *La Torre: Revista de la Universidad de Puerto Rico* 8.29 (1994): 25–49.

May, Georges. *L'autobiographie*. Paris: Presses Universitaires de France, 1979.

Mayhew, Jonathan. "Juan Gil-Albert's *Heraclés:* Homosexuality and Gender Identity in Twentieth-Century Spain." *Siglo XX/Twentieth Century* 11.1–2 (1993): 119–34.

Mayne, Judith. *Cinema and Spectatorship*. New York: Routledge, 1993.

McCaskell, Tim. "Euskadi: Out in the Basque Country." In *Coming Out: An Anthology of International Gay and Lesbian Writings*. Ed. Stephan Likosky. New York: Pantheon, 1992. 214–30.

Mercadier, Guy, ed. *Ecrire sur soi en Espagne: Modèles et écarts: Actes du IIIe colloque international d'Aix-en-Provence, 4-5-6 décembre 1988*. Etudes Hispaniques 14. Aix-en-Provence: Université de Provence, 1988.

Meyer, Moe. "Introduction: Reclaiming the Discourse of Camp." *The Politics and Poetics of Camp.* Ed. Moe Meyer. New York: Routledge, 1994. 1–22.

Mirabet i Mullol, Antoni. *Homosexualidad hoy: ¿Aceptada o todavía condenada?* Barcelona: Herder, 1985.

Misch, Georg. *A History of Autobiography in Antiquity.* Trans. Ernest Walter Dickes and Georg Misch. 2 vols. Cambridge, Mass.: Harvard University Press, 1951.

Moix, Terenci. *El beso de Peter Pan: Memorias: El Peso de la Paja 2.* Barcelona: Plaza y Janés, 1993.

———. *El Peso de la Paja: Memorias: El cine de los sábados.* Barcelona: Plaza y Janés, 1990.

Molloy, Sylvia. *At Face Value: Autobiographical Writing in Spanish America.* Cambridge: Cambridge University Press, 1991.

Monette, Paul. *Becoming a Man: Half a Life Story.* New York: Harcourt, 1992.

Moreiras-Menor, Cristina. "Ficción y autobiografía en Juan Goytisolo: Algunos apuntes." *Anthropos* 125 (1991): 71–76.

Morris, Barbara. "Almodóvar's Laws of Subjectivity and Desire." In *Post-Franco, Postmodern: The Films of Pedro Almodóvar.* Ed. Kathleen M. Vernon and Barbara Morris. Westport, Conn.: Greenwood, 1995. 87–97.

Mulvey, Laura. "Visual Pleasure and Narrative Cinema." *Screen* 16.3 (1975): 6–18.

Murphy, Ryan. "A Spanish Fly in the Hollywood Ointment: Gay Director Pedro Almodóvar Refuses to Be Tied Up by Censorship." *The Advocate* 19 June 1990: 36–40.

Murray, Stephen O., ed. *Latin American Male Homosexualities.* Albuquerque: University of New Mexico Press, 1995.

———. *Male Homosexuality in Central and South America.* New York: Instituto Obregón, 1987.

Navajas, Gonzalo. "Confession and Ethics in Juan Goytisolo's Fictive Autobiographies." *Letras Peninsulares* 3.2–3 (1990): 259–78.

Nelson, Emmanuel S. Introduction. *AIDS: The Literary Response.* Ed. Emmanuel S. Nelson. New York: Twayne, 1992. 1–10.

Ortega y Gasset, José. "Sobre unas «Memorias»." *Espíritu de la letra.* Ed. Ricardo Senabre. Madrid: Cátedra, 1985. 155–61.

Pally, Marcia. "The Politics of Passion: Pedro Almodóvar and the Camp Esthetic." *Cineaste* 18.1 (1990): 32–35, 38–39.

Paz, Octavio. *El laberinto de la soledad; Posdata; Vuelta a El laberinto de la soledad.* Mexico City: Tezontle, Fondo de Cultura Económica, 1981.

Perriam, Chris. *Desire and Dissent: An Introduction to Luis Antonio de Villena.* Washington, D.C.: Berg, 1995.

———. "Marginación y amor en la poesía de Luis Antonio de Villena." *Monographic Review/Revista Monográfica* 7 (1991): 135–45.

Perrin, Annie. "El laberinto homotextual." In *Escritos sobre Juan Goytisolo. Coloquio en torno a la obra de Juan Goytisolo, Almería, 1987.* Ed. Manuel Ruiz Lagos. Almería: Instituto de Estudios Almerienses, 1988. 73–81.

Persin, Margaret H. "Self as Other in Jaime Gil de Biedma's *Poemas póstumos.*" *Anales de la Literatura Española Contemporánea* 12.3 (1987): 273–90.

Petit, Jordi. *De hombre a hombre.* Barcelona: Icaria, 1984.

Piedra, José. "Nationalizing Sissies." In *¿Entiendes?: Queer Readings, Hispanic Writings.* Ed. Emilie L. Bergmann and Paul Julian Smith. Durham: Duke University Press, 1995. 370–409.

Plaza, Sixto. "'Coto vedado,' ¿autobiografía o novela?" In *Actas del IX congreso de la asociación internacional de hispanistas. 18–23 agosto 1986, Berlín.* Ed. Sebastián Neumeister. Vol. 2. Frankfurt am Main: Vervürt Verlag, 1989. 345–50.

Pope, Randolph D. *La autobiografía española hasta Torres Villarroel.* Bern: H. Lang, 1974.

———. "La hermandad del crimen: Genet examina a Goytisolo." In *Estudios en homenaje a Enrique Ruiz-Fornells.* Ed. Juan Fernández Jiménez, José J. Labrador Herraiz, and L. Teresa Valdivieso. Erie: Asociación de Licenciados y Doctores Españoles en Estados Unidos, 1990. 514–18.

———. "Theory and Contemporary Autobiographical Writing: The Case of Juan Goytisolo." *Siglo XX/Twentieth Century* 8.1–2 (1990–91): 87–101.

Preston, John, ed. *Personal Dispatches: Writers Confront AIDS.* New York: St. Martin's Press, 1989.

Prieto, Adolfo. *La literatura autobiográfica argentina.* Buenos Aires: Jorge Alvarez, 1966.

Puig, Manuel. *El beso de la mujer araña.* Barcelona: Seix Barral, 1976.

———. *Kiss of the Spider Woman.* Trans. Thomas Colchie. New York: Vintage, 1980.

Quance, Roberta. "Writing Posthumously: Jaime Gil de Biedma." *Anales de la Literatura Española Contemporánea* 12.3 (1987): 291–309.

Renza, Louis A. "The Veto of the Imagination: A Theory of Autobiography." In *Autobiography: Essays Theoretical and Critical.* Ed. James Olney. Princeton: Princeton University Press, 1980. 268–95.

Rodríguez Matos, Carlos A. *Llama de amor vivita: jarchas.* South Orange, N.J.: Ichali, 1988.

Roig Roselló, Antonio. *Todos los parques no son un paraíso (memorias de un sacerdote).* Barcelona: Planeta, 1977.

———. *Variaciones sobre un tema de Orestes (diario, 1975–1977).* Barcelona: Planeta, 1978.

————. *Vidente en rebeldía: Un proceso en la Iglesia.* Barcelona: Planeta, 1979.

Romera Castillo, José. "Autobiografía de Luis Cernuda: Aspectos literarios." In *L'autobiographie en Espagne. Actes du IIe colloque international de la Baume-les-Aix, 23–24–25 mai 1981.* Etudes Hispaniques 5. Aix-en-Provence: Université de Provence, 1982. 279–94.

Romero, Francisco. "El muro y la ventana: La 'otredad' de Luis Cernuda. *Cuadernos Hispanoamericanos* 396 (1983): 545–75.

Rose, Jacqueline. *The Case of Peter Pan; or, The Impossibility of Children's Fiction.* Philadelphia: University of Pennsylvania Press, 1993.

Rosenberg, John R. *The Circular Pilgrimage: An Anatomy of Confessional Autobiography in Spain.* New York: Peter Lang, 1994.

Rousseau, Jean-Jacques. *The Confessions.* Trans. and introd. J. M. Cohen. New York: Penguin Books, 1984.

Ruiz Lagos, Manuel. "Pájaros en vuelo a Simorg: Transferencias y metamorfosis textual en un relato de Juan Goytisolo: *Las virtudes del pájaro solitario.*" In *Escritos sobre Juan Goytisolo: Coloquio en torno a la obra de Juan Goytisolo, Almería, 1987.* Ed. Manuel Ruiz Lagos. Almería: Instituto de Estudios Almerienses, 1988. 169–228.

Russo, Vito. *The Celluloid Closet: Homosexuality in the Movies.* New York: Harper and Row, 1981.

Sahuquillo Vásquez, Angel. *Federico García Lorca y la cultura de la homosexualidad masculina: Lorca, Dalí, Cernuda, Gil-Albert, Prados y la voz silenciada del amor homosexual.* Alicante: Instituto de Cultura "Juan Gil-Albert"; Diputación de Alicante, 1991.

Said, Edward W. *Orientalism.* New York: Vintage, 1979.

Sarduy, Severo. "Explosion of Emptiness." Trans. Suzanne Jill Levine. In *Life Sentences: Writers, Artists, and AIDS.* Ed. Thomas Avena. San Francisco: Mercury House, 1994. 197–207.

————. "A Wart on My Foot." Trans. Carol Maier. In *Life Sentences: Writers, Artists, and AIDS.* Ed. Thomas Avena. San Francisco: Mercury House, 1994. 208–9.

Sartre, Jean-Paul. *Being and Nothingness: A Phenomenological Essay on Ontology.* Trans. and introd. Hazel E. Barnes. New York: Pocket Books, 1966.

————. *Critique of Dialectical Reason 1: Theory of Practical Ensembles.* Trans. Alan Sheridan-Smith. Ed. Jonathan Rée. London: Verso/NLB, 1982.

————. *Nausea.* Trans. Lloyd Alexander. New York: New Directions, 1964.

Schulman, Aline. "El nómada narrador en la obra de Juan Goytisolo." In *Escritos sobre Juan Goytisolo. Coloquio en torno a la obra de Juan Goytisolo, Almería, 1987.* Ed. Manuel Ruiz Lagos. Almería: Instituto de Estudios Almerienses, 1988. 45–58.

Sedgwick, Eve Kosofsky. *Epistemology of the Closet*. Berkeley: University of California Press, 1990.

Seidman, Steven. "Identity and Politics in a 'Postmodern' Gay Culture: Some Historical and Conceptual Notes." In *Fear of a Queer Planet: Queer Politics and Social Theory*. Ed. Michael Warner. Minneapolis: University of Minnesota Press, 1993. 105–42.

Shapiro, Stephen A. "The Dark Continent of Literature: Autobiography." *Comparative Literature Studies* 5.4 (1968): 421–54.

Smith, Paul Julian. *The Body Hispanic: Gender and Sexuality in Spanish and Spanish American Literature*. Oxford: Clarendon, 1989.

———. *Desire Unlimited: The Cinema of Pedro Almodóvar*. New York: Verso, 1994.

———. *Laws of Desire: Questions of Homosexuality in Spanish Writing and Film: 1960–1990*. Oxford: Clarendon, 1992.

———. *Representing the Other: "Race," Text, and Gender in Spanish and Spanish American Narrative*. Oxford: Clarendon, 1992.

Sontag, Susan. *AIDS and Its Metaphors*. New York: Farrar, Straus, Giroux, 1989.

———. "Notes on 'Camp.'" *A Susan Sontag Reader*. New York: Farrar, Straus, Giroux, 1982. 105–19.

Spadaccini, Nicholas, and Jenaro Talens, eds. *Autobiography in Early Modern Spain*. Minneapolis: Prisma Institute, 1988.

Spengemann, William C. *The Forms of Autobiography: Episodes in the History of a Literary Genre*. New Haven: Yale University Press, 1980.

Sprinker, Michael. "Fictions of the Self: The End of Autobiography." In *Autobiography: Essays Theoretical and Critical*. Ed. James Olney. Princeton: Princeton University Press, 1980. 321–42.

Stanton, Domna C. Preface. *The Female Autograph: Theory and Practice of Autobiography from the Tenth to the Twentieth Century*. Ed. Domna C. Stanton. Chicago: University of Chicago Press, 1987. vii–xi.

Swansey, Bruce, and José Ramón Enríquez. "Una conversación con Jaime Gil de Biedma." In *El homosexual ante la sociedad enferma*. Ed. José Ramón Enríquez. Barcelona: Tusquets, 1978. 195–216.

Teresa de Jesús, Santa. *Vida*. In *Obras completas*. Ed. Luis Santullano. Madrid: Aguilar, 1957. 53–257.

Thomas, Patricia Corcoran. *"La verdad de su amor verdadero": Gay Love and Social Protest in the Poetry of Luis Cernuda*. Diss. University of Minnesota, 1991. *DAI* 52.9 (1992): 3306A.

Ugarte, Michael. *Shifting Ground: Spanish Civil War Exile Literature*. Durham: Duke University Press, 1989.

———. *Trilogy of Treason: An Intertextual Study of Juan Goytisolo.* Columbia: University of Missouri Press, 1982.

Unamuno, Miguel de. *Autobiografía y recuerdos personales.* Madrid: Afrodisio Aguado, 1961. Vol. 10 of *Obras completas.* 16 vols. 1959–64.

———. *Niebla.* Ed. Germán Gullón. Madrid: Espasa-Calpe, 1990.

Van Leer, David. *The Queening of America: Gay Culture in Straight Society.* New York: Routledge, 1995.

Vargas Llosa, Mario. *El pez en el agua: Memorias.* Barcelona: Seix Barral, 1993.

Velázquez Cueto, Gerardo. "Para una lectura de *Un río, un amor* de Luis Cernuda." *Insula* 455 (1984): 3, 7.

Vernon, Kathleen M., and Barbara Morris. *Post-Franco, Postmodern: The Films of Pedro Almodóvar.* Westport, Conn.: Greenwood, 1995.

Vidal, Gore. *Palimpsest: A Memoir.* New York: Random, 1995.

Villena, Luis Antonio de. *Ante el espejo.* Madrid: Mondadori, 1988.

———. *Ante el espejo: Memorias de una adolescencia.* Barcelona: Argos Vergara, 1982.

———. *Corsarios de guante amarillo: Sobre el dandysmo.* Barcelona: Tusquets, 1983.

———. *Huir del invierno.* Madrid: Hiperión, 1981.

———. *Hymnica.* Madrid Hiperión, 1979.

———. *Poesía (1970–1984).* Madrid: Visor, 1988.

———. "La tentación del orden." *El País* 26 Apr. 1989: 13.

Walsh, John K. "A Logic in Lorca's *Ode to Walt Whitman.*" In *¿Entiendes?: Queer Readings, Hispanic Writings.* Ed. Emilie L. Bergmann and Paul Julian Smith. Durham: Duke University Press, 1995. 257–78.

Warner, Michael. Introduction. *Fear of a Queer Planet: Queer Politics and Social Theory.* Ed. Michael Warner. Minneapolis: University of Minnesota Press, 1993. vii–xxxi.

Watney, Simon. *Practices of Freedom: Selected Writings on HIV/AIDS.* Durham: Duke University Press, 1994.

Watson, Julia. "Unspeakable Differences: The Politics of Gender in Lesbian and Heterosexual Women's Autobiographies." In *De/Colonizing the Subject: The Politics of Gender in Women's Autobiography.* Ed. Sidonie Smith and Julia Watson. Minneapolis: University of Minnesota Press, 1992. 139–68.

Weeks, Jeffrey. *Against Nature: Essays on History, Sexuality, and Identity.* Concord, Mass.: Paul and Co., 1991.

Weintraub, Karl J. "Autobiography and Historical Consciousness." *Critical Inquiry* 1.4 (1975): 821–48.

"When the Gaze Is Gay." Spec. section in *Film Comment* 22.2 (1986): 31–50.

Whitam, Frederick L., and Robin M. Mathy. *Male Homosexuality in Four Societies: Brazil, Guatemala, the Philippines, and the United States.* New York: Praeger, 1986.

Winfield, Jerry Phillips. "Luis Antonio de Villena." In *Twentieth-Century Spanish Poets: Second Series.* Vol. 134 of *Dictionary of Literary Biography.* Ed. Jerry Phillips Winfield. Detroit: Gale, 1994. 334–45.

Winslow, Donald J. *Life-Writing: A Glossary of Terms in Biography, Autobiography, and Related Forms.* 2d ed. Honolulu: University of Hawaii Press, 1995.

Woods, Richard Donovon. *Mexican Autobiography: An Annotated Bibliography/ La autobiografía mexicana: Una bibliografía razonada.* Trans. Josefina Cruz-Meléndez. Westport, Conn.: Greenwood, 1988.

Wright, Les. "Gay Genocide as Literary Trope." In *AIDS: The Literary Response.* Ed. Emmanuel S. Nelson. New York: Twayne, 1992. 50–68.

Wyers (Weber), Frances. "Manuel Puig at the Movies." *Hispanic Review* 49.2 (1981): 163–81.

Yevtushenko, Yevgeny Aleksandrovich. *A Precocious Autobiography.* Trans. Andrew R. MacAndrew. New York: Dutton, 1963.

Yingling, Thomas. "AIDS in America: Postmodern Governance, Identity, and Experience." In *Inside/Out: Lesbian Theories, Gay Theories.* Ed. Diana Fuss. New York: Routledge, 1991. 291–310.

Young, Robert. "The Same Difference." *Screen* 28.3 (1987): 84–91.

Zimmermann, Marie-Claire. "Le moi et ses multiples noms dans l'oeuvre poétique de Luis Antonio de Villena." In *Ecrire sur soi en Espagne: Modèles et écarts: Actes du IIIe colloque international d'Aix-en-Provence, 4–5-6 décembre 1988.* Etudes Hispaniques 14. Ed. Guy Mercadier. Aix-en-Provence: Université de Provence, 1988. 189–211.

"Las zonas desérticas de nuestra literatura." *Revista de Literatura* (Madrid) 4.8 (1953): 261–63.

Adam, Barry D., 3

AIDS, 15, 17, 57, 61, 100, 104, 139, 147n2, 156n2; discourse, 121, 123–25, 127, 131, 133, 136; and Goytisolo, 122, 125–34, 136, 154n1, 155n13; and "homosexual body," 123, 136–37; inscription/description of, 15; writing, 121, 122–23, 148n4, 154n2

Almaguer, Tomás, 53

Almendros, Néstor, 127

Almodóvar, Pedro, 1, 14, 22, 23, 75, 106–18, 121, 135, 136, 138, 153–54; *Entre tinieblas,* 154n7; *Laberinto de pasiones,* 106, 107; *La ley del deseo,* 106, 112, 113, 153n4, 154nn7 and 8; *Patty Diphusa y otros textos,* 106–18, 153n4, 154n9; *Pepi, Luci, Bom, y otras chicas del montón,* 154n7

Alonso, Ana María, 6, 124

Anti-essentialism, 23, 40, 89, 138

Arenas, Reinaldo, 110, 154nn2 and 5

Arias, Consuelo, 148n8

Augustine, Saint, 8, 12; *Confessions,* 8

Autobiography (life writing): gay, 10–15, 22, 23, 25–71, 75, 76, 94, 106, 114, 117, 121, 135–36, 144n10; history of, 7–8; queer, 11, 13–15, 23, 73–118, 121, 135–36; in Spain and Latin America, 8–9, 143n7; theory of, 9–10. *See also* Confession; Diary; Heterobiography; Homobiography; Memoir

Babuscio, Jack, 83, 84

Barrie, J. M., 102; *The Little White Bird,* 96, 152n8

Basque Gay Liberation Front, 16

Bentham, Jeremy, 45

Bergman, David, 81

Bergman, Ingmar, 104, 153n14

Bersani, Leo, 5–6, 14, 27, 35, 110

Bianciotti, Héctor, 147n10

Binaries. *See* Homo(sexual)/Hetero(sexual) binary; Masculine/Feminine binary; Natural/Unnatural binary; Same/Different binary; Self/Other binary

Bios, 15, 121, 139

Blanchard, Marc Eli, 148n11

Blanco White, Joseph, 145n2

Body, female, 109, 111

Body, male: and Almodóvar, 110–12; in bourgeois ideology, 77; in cinema, 92–93; gay ("homosexual body"), 15, 82, 84, 123, 129, 135–41, 156n13; and homographesis, 11, 54, 136; straight, 84, 86

Bond, James, 97

Boone, Joseph A., 52

Boswell, John, 144n11, 145n20, 152n7

Brando, Marlon, 93

Brecht, Bertolt, 101

Burton, Richard, 147n11

Buss, Helen M., 15

Butler, Judith, 5, 81, 110, 156n1

Camp, 20, 76–77, 79, 81, 84, 95–96, 149n4; and AIDS, 104; and Almodóvar, 106–10, 114, 115, 154n5; attitude versus behavior, 95; and cinema, 92; eye, 77, 79, 95; and female body, 153n4; and Goytisolo, 130, 131; and Moix, 95–96, 104; and queer Spanish autobiography, 14; reverse of, 115, 130; and Villena, 78, 79, 81, 84, 87, 88, 138

Cañas, Dionisio, 60

Carrasco, Rafael, 3, 143n4

Castration: in psychology, 5; reverse anxiety, 113

Castro, Fidel, 44, 154n5

Castroite Cuba, 131

Castroite politics, 44

Catalán Gay Liberation Front, 17; *Manifiesto* of, 16–17

Catholic church, 27, 30, 32, 33, 35, 38

Cernuda, Luis, 18, 19, 20–22; "Alzate y vé," 22; "Dejadme solo," 21; "Noche del hombre y su demonio," 22; *Un río, un amor,* 20; "Todo esto por amor," 21

Cervantes, Miguel de, 98

Chacel, Rosa, 150n7

Cinema, Hollywood, 90–93, 96, 99; and homoerotic desire, 92. *See also* Film

Class: and queer theory, 5; social, 16, 77, 78, 91, 137, 143n5; struggle, 17; working, 17, 22, 53–54, 70

Clift, Montgomery, 93

Closet, the, 4, 19, 45, 98, 129

Index

■

ROBERT RICHMOND ELLIS
has previously published *The Tragic Pursuit of Being:
Unamuno and Sartre* and *San Juan de la Cruz:
Mysticism and Sartrean Existentialism*. He is a professor
of Spanish at Occidental College in Los Angeles.